WHEN WORK DOESN'T WORK ANYMORE

WOMEN, WORK, AND IDENTITY

Elizabeth Perle McKenna

Delacorte  Press

Published by
Delacorte Press
Bantam Doubleday Dell Publishing Group, Inc.
1540 Broadway
New York, New York 10036

The names and identifying characteristics of some of
the individuals in this book have been changed to
protect their privacy.

Library of Congress Cataloging in Publication Data
McKenna, Elizabeth Perle.
    When work doesn't work anymore : women, work, and identity /
by Elizabeth Perle McKenna.
        p.   cm.
    ISBN 0-385-31795-6
    1. Women—Psychology.   2. Women—Employment.
3. Self-perception in women.   4. Women—Identity.   I. Title.
HQ1206.M369   1997
305.4—dc21   96-38071
                                                            CIP

Manufactured in the United States of America
Published simultaneously in Canada

September 1997

10 9 8 7 6 5 4 3 2 1

BVG

For Steve,
Who knew

Acknowledgments

My deepest thanks go to the more than two hundred anonymous and pseudonymous women who spoke into the little recorder and to the thousand more who answered a very time consuming survey. You gave of yourselves without recognition and I hope this book has honored your lives.

Everyone should have a friend like Richard Pine—or an agent for that matter. He and his astonishing associate Lori Andiman never wavered in their wisdom, support, and belief. Their profound intelligence about publishing, and about life, infuse this book. I will never have enough words to express how important they are to me and how grateful I am to them.

I have been most fortunate to have been published by Dell, where I have been the recipient of brilliant and attentive publishing. To Leslie Schnur, friend, editor, and great publisher, my deepest gratitude. Jackie Cantor has been a terrific editor, full of ideas, energy, and wisdom. My thanks, too, to Carole Baron for her kindness and her belief in this book. Also at Dell, I want to thank the gifted Carissa Hayes, Tracy Locke, and Karen Mender. What a wonderful team they make. I have been in the best of hands with Lynn Goldberg and Camille McDuffie, publicists extraordinaire. To my Bantam Doubleday Dell friends Don Weisberg, Dave Lappin, Gail Browning, Mary Lange, Sally Johnson, and all my ex-colleagues in the sales department, thanks for having me back and listening to me one more time. And to Jack Hoeft, my deepest thanks for being a great mentor and longtime friend.

It's impossible to say how much Jane Isay contributed to this book. She is the discerner of the straightest line between two arguable points and the unswerving teller of truth, a great friend, and most gifted editorial sage. This book has been the beneficiary of her brilliance, and I am profoundly grateful to her. A thousand thanks, too, to Marilyn Abraham, who knows how to make books work and who helped me figure out what I was trying to say and the best way to say it. To Sue Wels, Adrian Allen, Christine Albertini, Lisa Queen, Stephanie Levi, Ann Patty, Hope Edelman, Susan Ginsberg, E.D., and Roger Straus III, who read this book or endured endless conversations about the subject, my deepest gratitude.

Enormous thanks go to Mark Levine, EVP Director of Strategic Planning for Wunderman Cato Johnson, for his invaluable and critical help with the research for this book. My thanks, too, to Michelle Smilek, who provided personal and sometimes technical support way above and beyond the call of duty.

I want to express my wonderment and gratitude to Anna Quindlen, Gloria Steinem, Letty Cottin Pogrebin, Janet Andre, Lillian Rubin, Juliet Schor, Idelisse Malavé, Elizabeth Debold,

Marie Wilson, Shelly Lazarus, Shoya Zichy, Rosalind Barnett, Susan Faludi, and Wendy Kaminer. These incredible women whose lives are full to overflowing never hesitated for a moment to share their knowledge and experience with me. If all the world would act in kind, this book would not need to be written. They are truly inspirational.

My father taught me how to write. A tough critic with the world's most tender heart, I can never thank him enough for all he has given me. To Yuen Yee Kee, thank you for being part of our family, for loving our son, and for teaching him your gentle heart. And to David, my thanks for not playing with my computer and putting up with Mama, shut up in a room, and not coming out for hours at a time. This is called work.

Finally, my deepest gratitude goes to my husband, who believed in me before I believed in myself and without whom this book would never have been written. I am the luckiest of women.

Contents

WHEN
WORK
DOESN'T
WORK
ANYMORE

Introduction

HERE IS MY STORY. IT IS EITHER A CAREER woman's fantasy or worst nightmare. In all probability it's a little of both. But one day, after years of dedicated work, pleasure from what I did, and a rewarding record of achievement, I walked into my boss's office and quit. The decision wasn't sudden, even if the action was. It had been a long time in the making. I was tired, depressed, and no longer enjoying a job I had once loved. To stay in my position I had been paying an increasingly heavy price in pressure, politics, and stress. I was losing perspective about what was important to me. The quality of my life was lessening at the same time that quality was becoming more important. I needed a break and I wanted to rethink what my priorities were. For years I had gotten everything I needed from work and I felt puzzled, betrayed, and frightened that my career now seemed to be the problem, not the solution. I knew I had to make some changes but I didn't want to give anything up. Certainly not my career, which was sacred ground and synonymous with who I was. But

1

there was less and less room for my "life"—whatever that was. If someone had told me then that giving up my professional identity would restore my love of work and then some, I would have asked them when they were released from the nuthouse. But that's what happened. It would take some time, though, before I discovered what enormous rewards were in store for me.

At least I wasn't alone in my dilemma.

Shortly after leaving work I picked up an issue of *Fortune* magazine. In it the editors had conducted a survey aimed at fleshing out the trend they perceived of widespread dissatisfaction of dedicated and accomplished career women—women like me who had ground slowly to a halt on the road of their dreams and needed to make some changes. "The generation of women that blazed new trails into the corporate suites is evidently blazing its own trails out," concluded *Fortune*.[1] The Yankelovich Partners survey of female managers and executives ages thirty-five to forty-nine found that fully 87 percent of the women surveyed wanted to make a major change in their lives. Forty percent felt trapped, close to 60 percent were in therapy, and 46 percent of these women over forty knew someone who was taking antidepressants.

Self-confidence wasn't the problem: 81 percent of the women responded that they were better at their jobs than most men. The glass ceiling wasn't the reason either: between 65 percent and 78 percent of the women expected to make significant advances in the near future. As to suppositions that women were leaving the fast track for hearth and home, the survey revealed no significant difference in the way women with or without children felt about their lives. Put simply, work wasn't working anymore for this accomplished group of women. According to the accompanying article, it seemed that the qualities of courage and ability that brought women to the top were the very same ones that were enabling women to stop, reevaluate, and, if necessary, redirect their lives.

Crisis at midlife, the article concluded. Perhaps. But lurking in the middle of the article was a statistic that seemed the lid to Pandora's box: *Three quarters of the women said they were defined by what they did.* Here was a group of successful women who wanted desperately to change what they were doing or how they were doing it. But if they were defined by what they did, how were they ever going to change their relationship with the work that was making them so unhappy?

This turned out to be my question precisely. Of course I identified myself by what I did. What was wrong with that? My career had been the most important part of my life for a long time. I also loved what I did and liked the people I saw every day. Sure, the corporate climate had changed; it was now totally bottom-line focused, more competitive, less loyal. But that was life, I figured. I was a career girl, pure and simple. Working met my financial, emotional, intellectual, and self-esteem needs. There were other things in my life, but work came first. Or at least it had for a long time.

I was one of those (probably annoying but commonplace) people who had always known what they wanted to do. I wanted a career, a successful career. A career as good as my father's. I rocketed out of college with a death grip on that first rung of the ladder of achievement. My ambition and later my position was my passport to the world. Financial independence had led to emotional independence. Through my twenties I concentrated on work. I worked at work, I flirted at work. Occasionally, I dated at work. I loved work and felt a puffed-up pride at having to spend a Saturday at the office; it made me important. At least in my own eyes.

There was a thrill in the chase of the next big promotion. There was power and purpose in getting to my destination. And there was preoccupation: I didn't have to pause and reflect; I had places to go, a person to become.

In my mid-thirties the road began to narrow a bit. The sales conferences in sunny Florida that had been glamorous and exciting were becoming inconveniently far away. The overnight sales trips no longer held the thrill of the road. I managed people. I was, by turns, a den mother, an advocate, and, increasingly, a martyr for their causes. And at thirty-five I absolutely, indisputably, felt the mortality of my ovaries. After all, I turned thirty-five around the time that a published study said I had as much chance of finding a husband as being blown up by a terrorist.

There had never been a rush to settle down. Suddenly, my friends who'd had their children in their twenties were now back in the career saddle. They seemed to have made a much better decision than I had. I had always wanted children. My mother had died when I was very young and to compensate for a lonely childhood I always had fantasies of a house full of kids running in and out. But it seemed that my daily "to-do" list just never got around to building a family. Sometimes, when I was suffering from a particularly bad day, I would chant, "Knock me up and drop me out." Even kidding, I looked at having kids as some kind of sabbatical from work. Everything revolved around my career. It was my creative outlet, my form of self-expression; it was me.

In my late thirties I married a man with a big job and teen-aged children. One of the great things we shared was our pride in each other's successes. We both had positions of responsibility and could commiserate about the pressures. On top of being life-mates we were peers. As a matter of fact, we had begun our relationship shortly after I went to him for advice on how to fire people. We understood each other on a professional level.

We negotiated a deal about kids—zero to one. And shortly before my thirty-eighth birthday, seventeen years into my career, I had a son. He showed up just about the time that I agreed to take on the biggest challenge of my professional life. But I could do it all. Others had. I'd just move some of my work life over to the side and slide the kid in. And I did it for a while. I just left the office a little earlier. I didn't take the trips I didn't have to. I skimmed proposals faster. My house was no showpiece. I cooked less, I slept less, but I was doing it.

I was no longer simply a publishing executive; now I was also my husband's wife, my son's mother. This complicated what I felt was expected of me, but I made no real changes in my daily activities. If anything, I clung a little harder to my work so I wouldn't lose myself in all those other roles. I didn't have an identity crisis, I told myself; I just had too much to do.

Because I'd been focused for so long on my profession, I had missed something very critical: the agenda I had set in place for myself in my early twenties had never been revised to take reality into account. Instead, as time went on and circumstances changed, I simply added more to my original list of things to be accomplished in my lifetime. The problem was that I valued my-self, I judged the worthiness of my life by progress toward the list's completion. My agenda included: college—check; career—check; husband—check; child—check. But when I created it, I was young and immortal and life had no consequences. Obstacles were just accomplishments in waiting. What I hadn't counted on was that embedded within the agenda were very different value systems and that much-sought-for perfect life couldn't possibly be achieved. As I proceeded down the checklist, I found I was feeling less and less good about my accomplishments because they involved more and more trade-offs in some inner, deeper valuing system that lay hidden within me.

In meetings these values started popping up dressed as yearnings for silence and sunshine. They made me crabby about going to business dinners I previously would have enjoyed. I wanted to put my son to bed. I'd rush out of a conference for a phone call from my husband, who traveled a lot, and I would miss whole conversations daydreaming about being outside during daylight hours. Because these fantasies jeopardized something that had sustained me for so long, I put my head in the sand and resisted their call. But I couldn't hide from the resulting erosion in the satisfaction I got from work. Whether I paid attention to what was going on inside me or not, things were definitely changing.

On the surface everything looked fine. Inside, however, I began feeling as though I was failing. I'd compare myself to other publishers who seemed to be devoting twenty-eight hours a day to their work. It was only time, I worried, until they discovered I was a fraud. I held myself up to other working mothers who seemed to be pulling off this home/work thing much better than I was. They actually got through sentences—even paragraphs—of conversation without having to bring up the latest cute thing their child had done. I'd look at the stay-at-home mothers who all seemed to be making pesticide-free baby food, reading all the child psychology books, and getting their children to eat broccoli without fisticuffs. I winced as I saw nannies wheeling babies down the street, knowing mine was one of them and believing what many people who wanted women out of the work world wanted me to believe—that he would have a better life if I were there for him all the time. And *everyone's* sex life was better than mine. I just couldn't get anything right, I felt, and my self-esteem was in the toilet from trying to be everything to everyone and ending up being nothing to myself.

Every message I gave myself about who I should be seemed right. Everything seemed equally and critically important. But these messages could not coexist. Something had to give and it was my peace of mind.

I had a work life. I had a personal life. Together, however, they made not one but two separate lives. Each wanted a hundred percent of me. I wanted one hundred percent of each. More important, both defined one hundred percent of me. Unfortunately, my self-esteem depended on succeeding in both lives equally well. I had been a working woman for longer than I had been anything else. I had standards for judging whether I was doing well or poorly. I knew, roughly, at any given point, where my stock was with myself and the world around me. I knew what I had to do to feel accomplished. I had standards about my home life as well. My marriage seemed solid (sleep deprived, but solid) and my son appeared undamaged by my daily departures. Okay, so I had brokered a provisional truce between work and home at the expense of some of my principles. But enough books had been written about the fantasy of "having it all" that I knew I was not the only mother whose high moral standards about banishing Barney from her house were easily swapped for a free half hour in which I could put in my contact lenses and locate a pair of intact panty hose.

Unbeknownst to me, however, I was judging my life by standards that weren't my standards and coming up woefully short. I had internalized these value systems over the years without knowing it and they measured the same fabric (my life) in completely different and mutually exclusive ways. There was the work standard, which told me that anything less than total devotion to my profession was failure. There were the voices of the women's movement that said, "Don't let us down. You can't drop out. You're a powerful example. Get in there, hang in there, and change things." Then there was society's measure of womanhood, which told me that the home was my first responsibility and that my child would be an ax murderer if I didn't make him my top priority. Everywhere, I read that if I worked too hard, my marriage would suffer. On paper these might be outdated concepts, but they weren't when I was growing up; they were the operative value systems and in creating a definition of a successful woman, I swallowed them whole.

The consequence was indigestion in my soul.

Of course, none of this showed up directly. I thought my problem was that I had a kid at a relatively advanced age and I had much more to lose than a twenty-year-old. In addition, I figured that I was just another working mother going through the tortures of trying to hold on to it all. While all that was true, that didn't account for the deepest levels of my discontent.

It wasn't that I was torn between two things I loved, I felt a profound loss in my relationship to my work. Like a marriage gone inexplicably but inexorably sour, I was mourning the loss of a love of my profession. Not the work. I loved the work. But it had simply become too exhausting emotionally and psychologically to keep working on terms that were increasingly not my own. I felt tremendous sadness as I saw that my most sustaining and enduring relationship—that of my career and me—had changed and was possibly ending. It would have been a critical mistake to conclude that motherhood was the cause or the solution of the problem. Motherhood was completely beside the point. All it did, really, was focus the problem—that I was working in a work environment that wasn't designed for a woman like me. A woman who wanted more than conventional success. A woman who wanted a life too.

When I saw my friends without husbands or children suffering the same angst I was experiencing, I realized something very fundamental was going on. It seemed *all* these powerful, bright women were feeling big holes in their lives. It didn't matter if they had kids or not. It didn't matter if they were married or not. All these women defined themselves as professionals, as workers. But work had stopped being enough for them too. A lunch wouldn't go by without one woman or another heaving a sigh, throwing her napkin onto the table, and saying, "I wish I could figure out something else to do." This statement would immediately be followed by a long list of why change was impossible, impractical, and irresponsible.

Here was an incredibly talented group of women. For the most part they were part of a generation who had been the chief beneficiaries of the women's movement.[2] They had been admitted to male universities. They became partners in law firms, vice presidents in banks. Those without children had gone from 50 percent to 95 percent of their male counterparts' earning capacity in a generation. They worked in a world where women in managerial and executive positions had to perform as well as men and where succeeding meant working as women on men's terms. Far from folding, the male business world simply added female poker players to the game. That meant that women sitting down to the table of opportunity and achievement played by the rules that had been in effect long before they got there.

Women compounded their lives by adding the male-defined success identity onto their female identities. For women to succeed, they had to learn to value themselves the way men did. They had to compare themselves to men while they competed with them. In doing so there is a subtle but consistent atrophying of the importance of other aspects of women's lives. As one real-estate executive said, "Anything that smacks of 'mom and apple pie' weakens my position in my industry. I have to compete with men on men's terms."

It's easy to bury the less immediately quantifiable, less success-oriented parts of life. There is no immediate payback for them. Indeed, those other roles of a woman's life can directly hinder her success. Women have fallen to the two–edged sword; by agreeing to be judged by the same rules as men, women put themselves in a position of denying or postponing whole parts of themselves. Women are warned by other women not to bring up "female" concerns. One publishing executive recently found out that her new boss wanted an 8:30 A.M. staff meeting every day. "I can't possibly get my daughter to school and be there in time," she worried. "I know this isn't the time to bring this up. It will look like I don't take my work seriously." And worse, women are faulting themselves for not being enough of what they don't even want to be. This takes a heavy toll emotionally.

But there comes a time when the neglected parts of our lives exact a price for this lack of balance. The symptoms range from old-fashioned burnout to boredom, an increasing sense of injustice or just plain old depression. The rewards from work stop compensating for a feeling of emptiness, wasted time, and a decreased sense of purpose and importance. These feelings get worse and worse and must be acknowledged and reckoned with—otherwise they can sour years of accomplishment. Once dissatisfaction sets in, the only remedy is to find some balance between work and the rest of life. The pendulum, having swung over the last forty years from the stereotypes of Donna Reed to Super Exec, seeks a resting place.

Compounding the need for equilibrium is the fact that women have worked very hard to get to managerial positions and while they have matured, they are tired. The generation of women who assumed they would be professionals is now hitting middle age. The go-go eighties took a real toll. For the first time balance is being seen as having value. Yet the workplace has remained remarkably unrehabilitated in its attitudes. Stereotypes still apply. In most offices motherhood is still a liability. And this isn't a problem just for married women with or without children; if any woman puts her "life" first—whether that life is mountain climbing or taking film classes—she isn't seen as "a contender." Most women, not men, end up leaving their jobs if they marry a co-worker. And if a woman is unmarried, she is assumed to be wedded to her job.

The struggle between the perfect résumé and the balanced life is waged unconsciously as well. Inside most women lie buried expectations and edicts about what being a woman is supposed to look like. We all had mothers to live up to or get away from. We have had decades of television telling us what we should be doing and how we should be doing it. Women still judge themselves as companions and mothers by standards that are not too far evolved from those of our grandmothers. No matter what shape a career woman's life takes, each one of these values has to be exposed and wrestled with at some point. And often the battle of the value systems shows up as work dissatisfaction.

Whether women want to marry or not, whether they elect to have children or not, they still must face the fact that fertility isn't forever. It's not accidental that the crisis of career is often coincident with the mortality of fertility. For many this awareness begins in their mid-thirties and is the first omen that life in the fast track ultimately terminates. For many it's the first time they realize that they aren't going to live forever or do everything possible under the sun. Because the workplace hasn't found a balanced way of incorporating "female" choices, the fertility question often has a real black-or-white feeling about it, creating a subtle but intense pressure.

My answer to this increase in internal friction was to ignore it as long as possible. But when I finally experienced a big reversal in my work, I had nothing to fall back on but my denial. The time had come to take some actions; like it or not, I had to make some changes, and because of the way work is structured I felt that I was being asked to choose between two extremes—meaningful work or some 1950s home fantasy—neither of which suited me or was realistic.

At four o'clock one morning, I sat in my darkened living room munching broken animal crackers. As I contemplated making a choice that would have profound consequences in my career, I was way too anxious to sleep. Inside my head I heard my father's voice telling me not to throw away my career. That was his value system. My husband's voice told me to stop anguishing and do something, anything, but to stop tearing myself apart. And from deep inside me I heard the voice of my mother telling me to lighten up. *I didn't get to live my life,* she said. *So don't waste yours in worry.* In this imaginary conversation I protested that I didn't know what was more important, work or home. *Think of how you missed me. Why would you want your son to feel the same way?*

This reverie revealed to me the deepest values that were particular to the holes in my life that I had been struggling to ignore. Discounting them meant constructing a life that guaranteed I'd be fighting myself constantly. Actually, I didn't like the message. It went against everything I thought I should be. It was terribly threatening. It meant shifting my priorities. It probably meant changing my career, because I couldn't do what I had always done in any meaningful way on a part-time basis or from my home. Those weren't options for me. But I clearly saw I wanted a more flexible life for a while. I didn't want to be asked to give up who I was as a professional and all I'd worked for. I resented the choice. But there it was.

Believe me, when I left my job, I had no idea that this hidden drama had been brewing just below the surface, informing my discontent. I thought I was unhappy because the management had changed or one thousand other things. A complete collapse of identity and crisis of values was not what I had in mind when I walked out the door. I thought my problems could be fixed with a new job and a few months of banging pot lids together singing, "The wheels on the bus go round and round." I didn't suspect that underneath my life's activities, my very soul had been torn to shreds from trying to be every woman I thought I should be. I still didn't know if I had done the right thing by leaving my job. I felt I had failed the women's movement, put a huge burden on my husband, let my father down, done the right thing for my kid, and jeopardized the bank payments on the new apartment we had bought two months earlier. And the immediate payoff was that I felt like a nonperson.

What I learned right away was that if I were going to be happy, I had to sever what I did from who I was. I needed an independent identity. My sense of self-worth had depended too much on my career. The first week without a paycheck I became worthless instantly. I was a three-legged stool and without a job to do every day, I toppled over.

I knew there were many women who had bumped through the same rocky transition from a work-based identity to one based on what was important to them. I'm naturally nosy and I began asking women I met what it felt like to change their lives. I'd sit in coffee shops, my son gnawing a bagel, and listen to the range of their experiences. Some women regretted the decision to stay home and missed their jobs passionately. Some cried as they dropped the baby off at day care. There were women who delighted in the mix of family and work. For other women without children my experience was a magnet; they were extremely curious to know what life was like "on the outside." "Oh, I would love to do what you're doing," sighed one publishing executive, "but I have no excuse [as in no child]." I countered that a very good mutual friend had just resigned her high-powered job and set off across the country with her husband. She didn't need a teething two-year-old to change her life. Just some financial planning and courage. Massive amounts of courage and faith that life was just as rich without the business card and all the things that went with it.

Each woman who had made the magical shift from being identified by her work to being just "who she was" had a story much like mine. It's crucial to say, however, that this is not a book about staying home with your kid. There are women in this book for whom that choice is hell. It would be absurd and beside the point to judge right or wrong. There is no right or wrong. That's the point. The issue here is the conflict itself, the tear between a life built around who we thought we should be as career women and who we have become in the process of our lives. Every woman interviewed in this book found herself at a point where the gap between what she was doing and who she was had gotten too wide to bridge anymore. Each had gone through a wrenching soul search about what was important to her and all had questioned whether they had the courage or the resources to make a change. Many had sacrificed material things in addition to job status. Others had risked stepping off the promotion path. Still others reveled in the freedom of movement and mind that had come from leaving a high-pressured corporate environment. The paths were as different as the women walking them. Some women found themselves recommitting to the work they were already doing. Others went into business for themselves. Some took time out or cut back on their hours, depending on what they could afford. Some, like me, switched careers and ended up pursuing lifelong dreams. And some had to stay in situations they didn't like for financial reasons, but they found a way to work with more peace once they changed their goals.

This is no small movement. Thousands of women with a great deal to lose are either planning on, dreaming of, or actually shedding old skins for new ones. Thousands have already gone through the process. These are women who love to work. These are women who have always worked. The women in these pages all pursued and continue to pursue careers. But most of them said that they had reached a point where they felt they were being asked to make a version of the choice I had to make—their careers or their peace of mind; their creative expression and independence or their lives. And since most of us have to work for economic reasons as well as psychological ones, this choice isn't really a choice at all but a sort of prolonged and somewhat hellish hypothetical.

Like me, the more than two hundred women interviewed and a thousand more surveyed for this book feel that there is a growing dissonance between their outer work lives and their inner values. This conflict is forcing an increasingly adversarial relationship between our work selves and personal selves. We don't want to be asked to choose between two parts of ourselves any more than we want to be asked to choose between outdated, old-fashioned, and gender-based lifestyles. The real tragedy in all this is that the very real love these women and I hold for our professions has become dwarfed by the maelstrom of bad behavior that results from increased corporate pressure, competition, and a punitive success and value system that is way too narrow to fit most of us comfortably.

When I left my job, I decided I wanted to write a book that tells the truth about what goes on in many women's working lives. This is not to say that there aren't many women for whom work is a sustaining joy. There are. And there are days when every woman in this book feels that way. But many of those women increasingly feel that they are working under compromising conditions. This is a book for women who feel that the way they work better fits a man with a wife at home to take care of life. This is a book for women who are struggling to rewrite their lives in midsentence so that the end of their stories involves balance and joy. Every woman I have talked to thirsts for the right mixture of stimulation and peace, of work and play, of time together and time apart. Most important, women strive for a harmony between who they are deep inside and how they live and spend their time.

Like most women I don't want to wait for my sixties and beyond to enjoy my life. Here, at the intersection of peak capabilities and confounding discontent, I want to make the choices that will give me the life that reflects who I am and what I believe in. I don't know what shape my tale will take, ultimately. But like the other women in this book, I now need to take some risks and go beyond the identity on my business card that sustained me for years. For I see now that identity has perversely narrowed my life and my options. I became so invested in "who I was" that I found it extremely hard to make room for "who I am."

17

In order to accept and enjoy my life I have had to better understand the forces at work within me and around me. I have had to honestly look at what I believe and what I value and what kept me working for so long without significant protest in an environment that is better designed for my father. Because it is my deepest hope and intention to work for the rest of my life, I have a lot invested in trying to see myself and the work world clearly. It's my only shot at a life of self-acceptance, wholeness, creativity, independence, and fulfillment. It's my only hope for meaningful change.

CHAPTER 1

Great Expectations

I WAS RAISED TO ACHIEVE, WHICH MAKES me a woman of my times. Born a Boomer, I adolesced as a hippie, achieved and accumulated as a yuppie, procreated as a thirty-something, and now, in the middle of my career, in the middle of my life, I find myself a member of the "anxious class." My incredibly prolonged process of growing up has been broadcast back to me from every possible angle through memoir, magazine, and, most omnipresently, television. At all times I have had pictures available of what I was supposed to be doing and when, how I was to dress for it, and how to recognize whether or not I was succeeding. At critical milestones in my life very detailed and specific cultural instructions and expectations were provided for me. All I had to do was pick up a magazine or newspaper, or turn on the little box in the corner of my living room.

As middle-class girls born after World War II, my friends and I were raised as heirs to a much anticipated abundance, the big "payoff" that would be the result of the sacrifices and strenuous efforts of our fathers and mothers. Our generation was repeatedly assured that not only was there a piece of the pie for everyone, there were going to be limitless numbers of pies. This promise of plenty infused my every sense of what was possible. In 1956, the year I arrived at Lenox Hill Hospital, more babies were born than ever before in history. Business was booming, the world was commuting, spaceships would soon orbit the planet. I had a dad who worked late, a mom who stayed home and made birthday cakes in the shapes of trains and elephants. I grew up with the World's Fair and its vision of the technological future, to the tune of the Beatles and the Rolling Stones.

I lived a life defined by possessions and appearances; I had my own room, record player, bicycle, allowance. I never knew a time without television, telephones, or instant cameras. My friends and I learned to dress alike, shop at the same stores in the same malls across the country, and eat food that tasted the same in Boise as it did in Bangor. In the small town where I lived, divorcées were still considered marked (and presumably miserable) women, cancer was discussed in a whisper as "the big C," and everyone had (or was supposed to want) a sibling, a dog, a dishwasher, and a fake-wood-paneled V-8 Vista Cruiser in the blacktop driveway.

I grew up seeing the link between protest and change. My television told me about demonstrations and demilitarizations, my teachers told me I could do any job a man could. And, in 1972, a law was signed that said I had a constitutional right to attend any college I wanted. In my short life I saw walls fall, roles reversed. I got the message: everything was mine for the asking.

Even though by birth order I placed in the latter half of the baby-boom generation, I was still a part of the sheer weight of numbers that first bent, then broke, convention and forever changed the expectations of women in Western culture. The sixties idealists were my role models as much as my parents were. Their dreams became my dreams became the dreams of the generation. We weren't going to look like or act like our parents. We certainly weren't going to live like them. We weren't going to dead-end in deadening jobs, we weren't going to stay home and make tuna casseroles. The men weren't going to have heart attacks or midlife crises; the women weren't going to be home alone and economically dependent or stuck in bad marriages.

It was all going to come together for me and my peers. We would live a life of endless success. Because of this certainty I failed to notice the stop signs and warning messages that flashed past me in my rush toward my life. I failed to notice them until I arrived at my destination, having lost a good deal of myself along the way.

Great Expectations

In 1961, when I was five years old, being a ballerina was a perfectly acceptable career goal (so was a princess, or more practically, a teacher and a nurse). It didn't really matter because it was assumed that I would get married anyway and spend the rest of my life raising my children and being a support to my husband. But by 1971 none of those assumptions applied. In less time than it took to buy, drive, service, and trade in a '65 Ford Mustang, all the expectations and opportunities for girls changed. I was a little

21

girl under one set of possibilities and a young woman under another. By the time my girlfriends and I bought our first training bras and got wired for braces, a revolution had occurred. No longer content with the narrower world of our mothers, we could now do the important things our fathers did. We were going to be doctors, lawyers, professors, investigative journalists, and rock stars. Only Janine Gold said she was going to be a wife and mother and have a really big house in the suburbs. But Janine Gold wore a sweater set to school and carried a real Gucci purse. She was a freak and we discounted her completely. We who were wearing hip-hugger bell bottoms with patches on the ass and no bras still had the wife-and-mother expectation but we just didn't focus on it. A family was a given, not a goal.

When I was in high school and about to apply to college, I asked my father what he thought I should do with my life. "You can do whatever makes you happy," he beamed. "You can be whatever you want to be." It was the same message I had heard at school and from the women's movement. I may not have had a mother, but my friends all did and theirs were urging them on to bigger and better lives than they had led. As a result we envisioned lives that included our father's accomplishments and our mother's connection and caring. In the course of our education our expectations were formed—there was nothing stopping us. We *would* do it all.

And for a long time we did. After all, as a group we enjoyed the longest adolescence in history. Where our mothers had married and given birth to us by twenty-five, we were using birth control, living with our boyfriends in our own apartments, getting our first promotions, or graduating from law school. We

worked in the same jobs with the same independence and opportunities as our brothers. Our work was challenging and interesting. And we started to taste the smaller privileges of the successful
life. I still remember the thrill of snapping down my first corporate credit card and finally being able to invite someone into an
office with a door that shut. (All right, it had been a supply closet,
had no window, and was directly behind the water fountain so I
worked to the hum of the cooler that went on and off all day. It
was still an office and it was mine.) It was exciting to make decisions about our work, help our peers, create and produce things
people needed or wanted. We traveled and built our own bank
accounts, clothed ourselves when and as we wished. Nested in
our own homes furnished as only we want them to be furnished.
We married later, had our children later, delayed our responsibilities. We experienced an affluence unimaginable in previous generations, both because of the economic times and because if we
had mates, we probably enjoyed two incomes. This wealth enabled us to use money to paper over problems. Because of our
demographic bulk we even muscled away the designated point of
middle age by a decade. Our early successes reinforced our sense
of invulnerability. We worked hard. We played hard. We identified ourselves by what we did. We valued ourselves by our contributions, our promotions, our potential. There was plenty of time
for the family stuff. Later.

Even though I'm now embarrassed to admit this, I really
thought that the rest of life was going to be like those immortal
days and that I would just keep adding to the wealth. I also
thought that I would be able to work when I wanted, not work
when I didn't. I believed I could keep a great job, do things that

would make the world a better place and still make plenty of money, have kids. I didn't worry about the consequences of decisions I was or wasn't making; consequences belonged to my parents' world, not mine.

Gloria Steinem laughs as I make this confession and wonders aloud whatever made the women of my generation think they could have it all. "If I had a dollar for every time we said you couldn't do it all, I'd be rich," she says with a shake of her head. "Look at me, I don't have it all; I never had or wanted children. And I know I couldn't have done what I have with my life if I'd had them." She and the other founders of the women's movement repeated over and over a message we chose not to hear as it flew in the face of our sense of endlessness: there was no way a woman could enjoy all the privileges of both the personal and the professional worlds. Not the way the worlds were structured. The economy depended on segregation and on the paid and unpaid division of labor. The family was built around it too. There were two different cultures, two different worlds. Two different identities. We could think of women's experience as an immigrant's, she suggested. If we want to fit into the male culture of business and success, we'd have to give up most of our own. Therefore, the goal was to transform that culture so both women and men could have family/personal lives *and* work.

But this is most definitely not the message I heard when I was younger and forming my expectations for my life. Like many of my friends I clearly got the feeling that not only could I do it all, but I *should* do it all. There was almost a moral imperative: to succeed at everything because we had been given these unprecedented opportunities. Opportunities for which world wars had been fought, class action suits filed. Opportunities our mothers wished they'd had. And we could do it. If we just worked hard enough. If we were good enough. It came as a confusing and anxious disappointment that in our thirties and forties, this world of satisfaction and fulfillment, with both intellectual stimulation and the warmth and comforts of home, hadn't come to pass. Instead, we found ourselves harried, in debt, and playing a sour form of poker that constantly forced us to trade a piece of life to get a piece of life. We found that all of the dream was possible only some of the time, and some of the time got smaller and smaller as our obligations at home and at work increased. And it felt worse and worse as the rewards themselves stopped compensating for the opportunities. We tried harder and harder with more and more variables to make everything come out as nicely and neatly as we had dreamed and expected. For a while we had led a perfect life. And when it started to become clear that we weren't going to have it all after all, we had no way to change our dreams and expectations without feeling we were going to lose something we valued deeply.

The Moment of Truth: The Baby Boom at Midlife

On a good day, when the bills are paid, when I know I made brilliant points in the eleven o'clock marketing meeting, when I haven't been eating to deal with my anxiety and my son has slept through the night, I am the luckiest person on earth to be able to do all the different things that make up my life. I feel vital and powerful. I am invincible. On a bad day, when every minute part of my life has someone's or something's name written on it, I am sure I will go crazy and end up on top of a water tank with an Uzi if I'm asked a question as simple as "Honey, have you seen my green tie?" In trying to navigate my life I feel as if I'm moving through an echo chamber where I am simultaneously hearing life instructions both from a very real present and a dreamy past I envisioned twenty years ago as I came out of college. I march forward to the music of this uneasy, discordant duet, trying to figure out what is "realistic" to expect of myself, my job, and others.

Understanding that "realistic" means accepting the consequences of choices we've made in our lives belongs to the wisdom of the weary. It implies a gut-level appreciation of compromise, an acceptance of real limits (internal and external), and a surrender to the clock. Three important conditions diverted us to "realistic" from the road that led to the perfect life: We matured and what was important to us started to change; we learned that the world of success still works best if you're a man with a wife at home or if you work like you're one; and we understood that the work world itself isn't what it was when we began our careers. We're heartbroken too. Most of us love what we do and none of us would trade our right to do it. But we don't like the way business works. We are increasingly sick of the petty politics, the unmanagable workloads. We are tired of working harder and harder with less satisfaction. We want to work more humanely, with more respect, recognition, and flexibility. We don't want to be penalized for wanting to have a personal life and we don't want to be asked to make all-or-nothing decisions about our futures.

Our personal lives, too, aren't exactly what we pictured growing up. Not only were we not supposed to be working so hard, but our husbands (if we had them) weren't supposed to be caught in the maw of the downsizing machine. Even if we had wanted a prince and the prince had come along, chances are he needed our income just as much as he needed his own. We quickly found that going to work also meant *having* to work. Quite apart from whether we wanted to or not—and most of us did—it just was a shock how quickly choice became necessity. Because many of us put our careers first, quite a few of us looked up in the middle of our lives and careers to find that we hadn't had time to get married or have children and that we had become our own safety nets. And those women who did start families not only had to perform all the tasks of their mothers, but their fathers as well. That's not exactly the picture we had in mind.

It's very difficult for women to discuss these disappointments. We think we will be judged whiners, political heretics, part of the backlash, or throwbacks to our mothers' generation. But when the topic came up in my interviews, after apologizing for herself, a woman would admit that she never really expected to have to be fully responsible for *everything* in her life, even if she thought she could do most of it. And she was exhausted from it. Even if her income wasn't the principal one, or the one that provided the benefits—and more than half the women surveyed said theirs was (which corresponds to other national polls[1]—because of the home she lived in, the car she drove, the importance of giving her children a good education, many women found their jobs were critical to having a life as good as the one they'd expected. None of these women said they wanted their mothers' lives; none wanted to go back to the dependent days. All said that their work had formed the core of who they were and the foundation of their self-esteem. Even if they didn't want to stop working, just the thought that they *had* to work made them feel trapped.

Sara Ann Friedman, author of *Work Matters: Women Talk about Their Jobs and Their Lives,* observed how her daughter Diana tries to reconcile her expectations:[2] "Yes, my daughter and women of her generation juggle and struggle. Yes, she is angry and frustrated and longs for more time. Yes, she is of a generation disillusioned—denied both the myth of glorious, totally fulfilling motherhood and the myth of the have-it-all supermom. And yes, she works because she has to. But that need is psychic as well as financial; her work is an integral and permanent part of her life. Her world, with opportunities, desires, and possibilities inconceivable to even educated women years ago, is galaxies distant from mine at her age. And for Diana and women of her generation the jig of self-delusion is up. For they know, as we did not, that their choices are more illusion than reality. They also know that while the problem of balancing work and family may be theirs to solve, the blame for finding themselves in an all-but-untenable situation does not lie at their doorstep; the fault is not their inadequacy, their selfishness, nor their desires and ambitions unbefitting a female. Even though everything has changed, nothing has changed."

This is the reality for the baby-boom generation as we hit midlife. Everything has changed, nothing has changed. We may have changed much in the world, but we haven't made much of a dent in the work culture. Now the youth culture is three decades beyond the Kill-everyone-over-thirty maxim, and we are simultaneously hitting both the middle of our lives and the middle of our careers. The rules of business start to chafe us and the values—which might have made sense for the way our parents lived—don't represent what is important for us today. As we approach the point where our career growth curves flatten to a limited horizon, we also see that our lives have edges. With the perspective of our experience we see that we aren't ever going to have it all, that Gloria Steinem was absolutely right. We come to this point having brokered a life of subtle trade-offs that, cumulatively, haven't landed us where we'd hoped. We've become successes without the pleasure we thought would accompany that accomplishment. With the clarity that comes from experience, we see we will have to make some serious changes in our lives and the systems around us if we want fulfillment. Before it is too late.

We see that even though our lives differed greatly from those of our parents, the institutions around us haven't changed as much as we have. It took us a few decades to discover that even something as seemingly innocuous as the fact that orthodontists keep the same hours as bankers signals a clash of expectations, roles, and values—the ones installed in us as young women and the ones we developed along the way. On some level society still expects and wants that woman banker to be home to take her kids for braces. And on some level she expects and wants to be there too. On another level society expects her to be present at the three o'clock marketing meeting. As does she. If she takes the afternoon off and goes, her work is compromised. If she can't get there, the kids are compromised. Chances are, she will feel guilty for either absence. Or she'll be angry because she gave up a chance to show up for her kids and she won't get that promotion she hoped for anyway. Even if she did get the promotion, it would only be an opportunity to work even harder.

Experiencing the reality of these conflicts didn't come with our entry-level jobs; it took time to develop. By the time we hit this point, most of us have invested a great deal in our lives; we may have ten, fifteen, twenty years of working behind us. We feel too burdened, too scared, to change. As our horizons contract and our gum- and hairlines start to recede, improbably, we also find ourselves at the peak of our careers. The alternatives—or lack of them—become painfully clear. In trying to get a handle on what to do, some women are tempted to resurrect in rosy retrospect the simpler way we used to live in which men worked and women cared. But most women, having won the right to work, having proved that they can succeed, having enjoyed the intellectual challenge, the freedom of expression, the corporate expense accounts, the self-empowerment, wouldn't dream of not working. After all, our very identities are based on what we do. But now, in the middle of our careers, we are spending a great deal of time wondering about how else we could be spending a great deal of time. It's making us take a good hard look at what we value and how we live.

We are finding that what is important to us is shifting. As we get older, we don't need the identity on our business cards or the accessories of success as much as we want the more enduring (but less objectively defining) values of friendship, family, serenity, and leisure time. Whether propelled by outer circumstances or inner turmoil, women are stopping and reassessing what is important to them and what they can do about it before it's too late. Every woman's story told a version of that, but none was more clear than Jane's.

When What Is Important to Us Changes

Everyone who knows Jane calls her one of the sanest people they have ever met. She's the kind of person you go to for a referral to a really good restaurant, a really good doctor, and for really great advice. She rarely acts out, she enjoys a good laugh, good food, and good company. She's a terrific stepmother to her two stepchildren and an attentive daughter to her aging parents. She takes things in stride in her own time, and, for the most part, on her own terms. And, at forty-five years old, she knows herself very well.

"I am, perhaps, one of the most risk-averse people I know," she admits. "And security is very important to me. Security for the future, that the money will be there, that we'll be okay even if there's another depression. I've never been a self-promoter, it's not in my nature."

Jane also loves the editorial work that has been her occupation for twenty-two years. "It started out as a summer job—*everything* is a summer job when you're twenty-two." She laughs when she's asked when that summer job became a career. "It became a career by the end of the summer. I knew that I wasn't going anywhere else. This was the best thing I ever did. I had a terrific boss who was a real classic mentor. He would stick things in front of my nose and ask, 'Do you know what this is? Do you know what that means?' It was much more fun than being in school, which was the only thing I knew how to do. It was stimulating. There was a whole community of bright people my age and we were all in it together."

Work gave Jane a charge. She worked all the time. She had to reassure her father, who was more worried about her working all the time than about her lack of a husband, that *everyone* she knew worked all the time. She loved it. She didn't have a television or a stereo, and she only dated men who weren't marriage material. It wasn't until she bought her own home at thirty-four ("Of course I had the money; I worked constantly and never spent money on anything") that her life began to gradually open up. She became a scuba diver and started fixing up her home. It so happened that that period was also the happiest time in her career. "Not only did I edit books, but I was writing articles which were being published around the country. I kept getting tear sheets of my articles from this or that paper, which gave me a real kick. I also pushed my company into publishing cookbooks, and because we were dissatisfied with the jacket art we were getting for them, I took over the art direction and styling of the photographs. It was a wonderful time in my life. I had all these different things going on. It was a very creative and fulfilling period, It was also a time where I was identified almost totally by what I did for a living."

Jane's career was marked by an orderly, steady progression to increased responsibility, larger jobs, and new publishing houses. It was the late 1980s and the industry was being changed rapidly by a seemingly nonstop series of acquisitions, where independent publishing houses were being bought by larger and larger media corporations. "I like to tell this story," Jane says, sighing. "When I was twenty-two, I worked for the editor-in-chief, who, in turn, worked for the head of the company. Twenty-two years later I was a vice president and editor-in-chief of a seventy-nine-million-dollar division. I worked for a president and publisher who, in turn, worked for a group president who worked for a CEO for the group who worked for a corporate executive vice president who worked for . . . You get the picture."

For Jane it signaled the end of the community and therefore the end of communal purpose. "The work became increasingly purposeless," she said with sadness. "I didn't want to move on to the next level. I liked what I did and was happy doing what I was doing, but I just didn't want to be doing it in an increasingly meaningless way. I couldn't devote enough attention to publishing three hundred titles a year and be involved with the acquisition of seven hundred more books. I went to three editorial meetings a week and seemed to live in meetings. I really felt I wasn't doing it any better, I was just doing it thinner. I was more spread out."

Jane began to feel she was going through the motions and running harder just to stay in place. She saw editors who year after year produced stunning best-sellers for the company only to receive little more than a pat on the back and be asked immediately, "What's next?" She watched her company swallow a second company and be swallowed in turn by a third, bigger company all within one year. She started to want more quiet time. She and her husband took more and more vacations away from it all, far out in nature. It began to dawn on her that the whole point of their lives had become supporting their lifestyle. This really didn't make sense to her. "It had no substance and it was really like a cat chasing its tail. It didn't go anywhere or get us anywhere. It didn't raise the intellectual quotient any after a while. It didn't make us smarter. It certainly made us nuts. We would work like morons all week and go to our weekend house, for which we were paying a fortune, and drop dead like two sacks of flour. We were so numb, we couldn't even speak. It got out of control. We were working harder and enjoying it less."

A huge part of Jane's growing disillusion related to the growth of the corporation. She felt there was a direct correlation between the size of the companies she worked for and the decrease in her satisfaction. "The human factor," she states, recalling Graham Greene. "Don't forget about the human factor." What had started out as an exhilarating community of wonderful people with a common goal had become a huge dinosaur with a little brain all the way up at the top telling the left toe what to do. "Look at the imprint I ran," she said with disgust. "We went from forty-three million dollars to seventy-nine million dollars in four years. Was anybody excited about this? Once a year at sales conference somebody would get up and make a speech." For Jane, as the recognition and shared sense of purpose dissolved, her motivation and joy in the work began to flag.

Jane began to feel undervalued and underappreciated. Because of the increasing layers of hierarchy, she found she had increasing amounts of responsibility and decreasing amounts of authority. Someone was added to her staff without her having been so much as consulted, and she, in turn, had to fire the employee after a year of time-consuming training proved fruitless. She had the responsibility of firing the employee but not the authority to decide if the employee belonged in her department. She found she couldn't solve simple problems without going through several layers of approvals. Promoting people or reorganizing them became a beast. Budgets were cast in stone and she found she could no longer effectively improve the quality of the lives of her employees. She grew cynical, and while still a "team" player, she started to withdraw and become depressed.

There was no moment of epiphany for Jane. Her decision to make a major change in her life rolled out over several months and a lot of it had to do with people around her dying. In one fall she lost a friend to colon cancer, another to stomach cancer. Her neighbor died of AIDS, her husband's ex-wife succumbed to ovarian cancer. A sales rep died of a brain aneurysm, as did a literary agent friend. These were all women under fifty-five years of age and it frightened Jane. "It was during that fall that I was surrounded by death and I was sick with pneumonia myself. I started to feel there had to be more to my life. I wanted more purpose and texture to it. It also came to me that despite the job, despite the title, despite the money, I had the sneaking suspicion that I was underachieving for the first time."

As if that weren't enough, Jane watched as her husband was edged to the side and then forced out of his company after twenty-five years. "He helped build that company," she said, her voice still carrying resentment. "And then, a new management, and finito. It was disgusting to watch and I was terrified about what would happen to this man who had given so much of himself to this company for so long. It was scary and heartbreaking. And it made me sick."

She and her husband started to think about starting up or

buying their own book-publishing or packaging business. "Some-place where we could make a difference again. Where our work would have purpose and meaning and where we could contrib-ute." The seed was planted and they began fantasizing about what it would be like to move out of New York, out of their current lives. "The whole thing took on an almost gamelike quality," she said. "If this happens, then we do that. We would sit around with a map and ask ourselves where we wanted to live and how we could do it."

Six months later, after careful financial planning, Jane quit her job and she and her husband set out on the road, leaving behind a collective fifty-two years of corporate life. "Part of it was leaving something," she says, "and part of it was going to some-thing. What I envision is not radically different. But I want a richer life, one with more threads in it. The thread got very thin and monochromatic after a while. I thought I was weaving a giant tapestry of different interesting people and different interesting books. But what I was really doing, at the end of the day, was feeding the machine. I want to bring back the feeling of working on a tapestry. I got so close so gradually that all I could see was the red. I couldn't see anything anymore. Now maybe I'll learn something new, try a new thing."

When Jane left, they threw a wonderful party for her. She felt great about leaving. "I had a great run," she said, smiling. "And I ended it with dignity."

Many women I have talked with have told a version of Jane's story. Jane knew exactly what was going on in her life and she watched it grind down over a long, slow period. Her love of her profession may have stayed constant, but the working environment changed radically enough that for Jane to remain in her position, she would have felt worse and worse about herself. Corporate consolidation, more responsibility, lessened authority, all added up to more work with less quality in a dehumanized atmosphere. As other things became more important to Jane, it became harder and harder to put up with the politics and pressures of work.

It would comfort Jane enormously to know that her feelings make her a candidate for poster child of her generation. In February of 1996 *The New York Times* devoted six consecutive front-page stories detailing the loss of faith American corporate workers have in their corporations. A 1993 Roper Starch World Wide poll found that two thirds of professional women's view of success had changed and another two thirds of them agreed that making money wasn't as important to them as it had been five years earlier. In 1995, a survey for Deloitte Touche, LLP showed only 2 percent of professional and executive women were very satisfied with their work.[3] Only 7 percent of those women said they were in it for the money. When conditions make it difficult to do good work, women like Jane find themselves feeling increasingly demoralized. The very passion for the work ebbs. They often sink to a lower level of performance, which in turn lessens their self-esteem. In short, nothing makes up for it, not money, not promotions. The only answer becomes working differently and under very different conditions. The problem is that those different conditions usually aren't going to pay as well as corporate jobs. Women end up facing a choice between their lives and their *lives*.

On average these women have twenty more years to work.

Many of them say they want to jump out an office window at the thought—if only they could get it open. For them the thrill of the chase toward the goal has often turned into the grind of the routine. The career ladder has narrowed, there are fewer opportunities. We see those that do exist too often go to less qualified men. We begin to question "whether it's worth it." We begin to reevaluate what's important and try to figure out what we want for the next half of our lives. Over the years, just as Jane did, we have held high standards for ourselves and our work. But when the office environment frustrates good work or makes it impossible, emptiness, frustration, and depression step in.

Many women settle in at this point and just accept that "that's life." Others decide to change their relationship to and attitudes about how they work. Some, like Jane, decide actually to change the circumstances of the work itself. All have to figure out who they are and what their own definitions of success are (apart from business achievements) in order to renegotiate the emotional contract they have made with their careers. And no matter what the decision, there are trade-offs.

But when it starts to dawn on us that we aren't immortal, the stakes ratchet up a notch. Barbara Ehrenreich, sociologist and award-winning author, says, "There is a clear generational reason why women are beginning to take a more jaundiced view of conventional success: America's pioneer fast-track businesswomen are hitting midlife and their own version of the famed midlife crisis." She continues: "Meaningful work and a balanced life are deep rooted and genuine human needs. Like any needs they can be repressed or ignored for years at a time, but sooner or later they're going to assert themselves."[4]

As Jane began to experience the vulnerability of mortality, her priorities changed. What was important to her changed. How she valued her time, her life, and her relationships changed. All the while her outer life stayed more or less the same. Jane, the self-admitted queen of stasis, found she was more afraid of what would happen if she didn't make some changes than if she did.

Jane's story pointed my search in the direction of the critical values of balance and fullness. It helped to spotlight how misshapen the fabric of our lives can become when we go to work in a man's world if we do that work as women working on male terms. The work world may have let us in, but for all our idealism we haven't changed how it operates or the rewards it offers. The working world remains a segregated place. A place built for men with full-time wives at home to take care of the rest of life. It is built around men's need to be defined and valued by what they do, not who they are. Along with the opportunity to work with men, side by side, comes their value system and a way of looking at ourselves and judging whether or not we are doing okay. That explains why many women say that having performed tasks assigned, they are outwardly successful and inwardly wanting.

But we've come so far and we don't want to go back to the world of our mothers. Work is vital to us. We need and want the independence and fulfillment it offers. There is nothing wrong, most of us say, with the content of our work. But the context and form need radical revision if it's to fit in to our lives today in a balanced way. We are not our mothers. That postwar, affluent generation, a hiccup in history, has set up, in the work world, an unrealistic structure that is suited only to a tiny portion of the world's population.

There is plenty of time to change in the middle of our journeys. We can take control of our lives. Midlife and midcareer aren't exact points in space but attitudes and feelings. We can make new contracts with our jobs and begin how we work all over again right in the middle of what we are doing. The process of changing ourselves and our lives, however, is neither painless nor orderly. We wander between boundlessness and boundary, feeling big one minute and tiny the next. It's hard to let go of immortality.

So, without map or precedent, this generation of women is setting sail through turbulent waters where we hope to find the freedom both to work and to enjoy our friends and families without penalties. Our ships, however, are made of old lumber; we can't change the fact we constructed them with the values and assumptions installed when we were girls. They act as silent navigators who invisibly seek to steer our course and judge our progress. In order to see clearly, we have to understand their encrypted instructions to us.

CHAPTER 2

When Work Becomes Identity

By the time my braces came off, the message was already very deeply implanted in my gray matter: The good life came either from having a successful career of my own or settling for the next best thing and marrying a guy who had one. No one talked much about wife-in-training skills by the time I started work, although they had quietly shadowed the rest of my education like a just-in-case cloud. These mixed signals created some very skewed pictures inside me. My aunt and grandmother showed my cousin Ginger and me how to cross-stitch and needlepoint. My uncle concentrated on teaching us skiing and fishing. My dad helped me to swing a golf club and a tennis racket. I witnessed the importance of being a supportive listener, a pretty dresser, a gourmet cook. These were the women who got my father's attention and he was, I learned, something very valuable—a successful man.

It became apparent that how I looked had a good deal to do with my future (or lack of one) in the success department. The extra twenty pounds I brought home with me after my sopho-more year—the result of eating my way through academic and social angst—produced something close to a state of panic in my dad. For no matter how many A's I brought home, if they came swaddled in spare tires they weren't much good. Even though I was told I could be what I wanted to be, do what I wanted to do, unspoken in those encouragements was the conviction that pro-fessional success notwithstanding, society would still judge me by my ability to attract a man and by what kind of wife and mother I turned out to be.

Even though we worried about our weight, clothes, and dances, for the most part the girls in the class of '74 focused on accumulating measurable accomplishments and getting good SAT scores. We quickly gleaned that any hopes for increasing opportu-nity grew best in the fertile culture of personal achievement. We were raised to evaluate ourselves by our accomplishments. Being the best people we could be, we learned, could be easily and objectively measured, first by the kind of grades we brought home, then by the college degree we were awarded, the attrac-tiveness and financial promise of the men who accompanied us to Thanksgiving dinner, and, ultimately, by the title on our business cards and the perceived importance and the financial rewards of the work we did.

We knew what success looked like—we had to get married like our mothers and have careers like our fathers. By the time we graduated from college, my friends and I were completely sure that our happiness, success, and our very identities would depend on our own efforts in our own lives and not those of our hus-bands. We also knew that without privileges or good financial rewards, work was just that—work. We wanted more than that. We wanted work that had meaning and importance—work that made a contribution. And we wanted to succeed as our fathers had succeeded. *That* was our definition of work that worked.

It never occurred to me or any of the women I knew growing up to challenge our culture's love affair with this rather narrow and extremely materialistic picture of the classically successful life. Sure, we'd had our sixties ideals, but even Jerry Rubin was working on Wall Street by the time I graduated from college. I assumed that having money paved the path to a happy life and would open a world of independence and freedom at my feet. A "good job" meant travel, a vice presidency, and having enough money that I'd never have to depend on a husband even if he could afford to provide for me. Success would be marked by having a corner office thirty-two floors above Sixth Avenue and Fiftieth Street in Manhattan with a rust-colored suede couch and matching chair. As my father sat at his desk surrounded by testimonials to him, scotch in hand after a hard day, it was apparent to me that success was the finest fruit of the tree of opportunity. It endowed a special identity and status. To me my father's success was so bright that I lived by its reflected light. I could tell my friends' parents what my father did and see approval in their eyes, not just of him but of me too. It was very clear that his success defined him and took care of me. In return he gave his career his all.

From my father I learned about the values of success. Having it ensured stability, acceptability, surety. Success was a strange combination of power, duty, and self-sacrifice. I saw that even when he felt trapped by his work and responsibility, my father persevered. Rather than fault the situation, I learned, instead, to admire the character of a man who hung in there and sometimes triumphed under stress. I learned that the nights away from home and late evenings at the office were part of the bargain made for identity and security. A price my father seemed content to pay, a price he expected to pay. My father went to work as a form of love—to give me a better life than he'd had, to give me everything I wanted or needed. I appreciated the trade: my father's physical presence withheld for the noblest of causes—my happiness and well-being. I believed that his success and the quality of my life were deeply linked. I saw that it was okay for work to be important. Just as important as I was.

Far from challenging that model I, like many other young women, wanted to triumph at it so I could break down its exclusivity, enjoy its privileges, and achieve the benefits on our own. In the beginning of our careers, when we had no responsibilities other than ourselves, we threw ourselves into our work with the same passion we brought to our love affairs. It was exciting going to the office every day. We apprenticed with people we wanted to please. We were rewarded with new assignments, increasing responsibility, and autonomy. We started to have an impact. We felt part of something bigger than ourselves. While we were enthralled with this exciting stage of infatuation, it was unnecessary to question anything. Indeed, work was our proving ground for becoming adults. And as long as we valued ourselves and judged our progress by the conventional tokens of achievement—raises, promotions, increasing levels of responsibility—there was no need to have any distance from what we did. There was no apparent downside; there was only the picture of success. "The biggest

mistake the women's movement made," Jane said, "was not challenging the male system of success. We went to work, we chased
the goals, we didn't question the values. We even put on those
silly little suits." We didn't focus on the fact that it would be
harder and harder to sustain that success as we broadened our lives
outside of the office. We were young and immortal and in love
with our jobs, we didn't see that the nature of the workplace and
the demands of a successful career hadn't changed, they'd only
gone coed.

Simultaneous with the baby boom's entry in force into the
world, the women's movement itself entered a new stage. "What
happened to women and work took a very specific turn in the
early seventies," says Idelisse Malavé, the former vice president of
the Ms. Foundation, now head of the Tides Foundation. "Main-
stream feminism took a turn to equal-rights feminism. 'We are all
equal,' it said, 'which means that if you have X, then I can have
X.' Which was fine. The place that it was skewed was that it was
saying that whatever the dominant class had then, that was the
thing to want, which is the hallmark of oppression. It's like we all
bought into the oppression at some level. It was okay to say that if
men work, then women shouldn't be denied the opportunities
that men had. But we did this without a great deal of reflection.
We did this without asking, *Is that what I want? Is that something
worth wanting?* It's like looking at rich people and assuming everything that they have is great. Well, a lot of what they have is great.
And a lot of what they have isn't."

So we went to work aiming for success. And a lot of it was
great. And a lot of it wasn't.

Achievement

No one knows that better than Ellie Daniels. Ellie's job as a vice president at a major brokerage house has taken her all over the world. It has bought her a home of her own, provided for her retirement. It has paid her for ski vacations, summer homes, and allowed her to support some charities that mean a great deal to her. When asked about what success means to her, she laughs. "I bought it. I bought the whole career thing. I felt very disempowered by my father, who used to say charming things like 'If we ever run out of money, only the boys are going to college. It's not as important for you girls; you can always get married.' I think, at some level, my career has been about proving him wrong as much as proving I'm right. So I went for the biggest, meanest industry in the biggest, meanest town and I conquered. And while I feel pretty great about that, I also know that success kicked the shit out of me. And that's the truth."

Ellie is like many of the other women I interviewed who focused their expectations for fulfillment, recognition, and self-definition largely on their careers. Like so many women who entered the working world in the late seventies and early eighties, she had only male mentors and role models. Ellie liked the picture their success painted and she wanted it for herself.

Not that Ellie planned to be a Wall Street investment banker. Growing up in the midwest, she didn't even know what one was. Instead, Ellie started out after college in one of the two fields she was told were appropriate for women: nursing and teaching. Since she hated the sight of blood and loved to go camping with eight-year-olds, Ellie became an elementary school teacher. "I was," she admits, "the Accidental Careerist. If I hadn't gotten sick and tired of making endless copies of balls, bats, and mittens, I'd still be living in Montana, probably fat and happy."

But Ellie got both bored and concerned about her future—a bad combination and one calling for a serious change of course. "I couldn't imagine myself five years out working on mittens," she recalls. "And I realized that no white knight was coming along. I wanted more money and security and I figured that I was just going to have to go out and get it. I suppose if I had been five years older, I would have gone to law school because everyone seemed to be going to law school. But I looked around, and everyone was getting their MBAs, so I did too."

Ellie's timing couldn't have been better. She graduated with a degree in finance in the early eighties, figuring she'd go into some public service administration. "But these really amazing guys were coming through with the suspenders and the blue shirts with the white collars and the beautiful ties. They were From New York. They were Investment Bankers. I had no idea what an investment banker did. But I sure liked the way it sounded. They were trying to recruit women; I was one of those, I fit the bill." Ellie set off for Chicago and the beginning of what would become a fifteen-year run.

"It was perfect for me!" she exclaimed. "I was an overachiever, a perfectionist, a workaholic, and I had very low self-esteem. All of a sudden I was 'in the pack.' I killed myself and got fabulous reviews. I got paid a lot of money and I loved it. It felt like I was getting affirmed by this corporate environment. The money was not as important as the reviews, though. What was critical was the validation, the excitement of playing on the same field as the big boys." Ellie's success gave her confidence and a sense of control over her life. It seemed, too, that there was no end to what she could hope for.

The Unwritten Rules of Success

When we went to work wanting the success Ellie wanted (and got) we didn't see limits, we saw only possibility, achievement, excitement. We wanted to learn skills, make friends, become proficient in our professions. We wanted to achieve things in our lives. But we learned something else on the road to career success. We didn't see that achieving the success of our mentors actually meant that we would start complying with a certain system of behavior that governs the way most businesses work. Like Ellie we had to learn this complex and hidden set of rules if we wanted to get the interesting assignments, the good salaries, or even to have job security.

This set of rules reflects the male culture that created them, and achieving any real success is very hard without obeying them. We may not have been aware that there was a cultural difference at work in our climb up our organizations but, once we had been working for a while, found that we didn't quite agree with some of these rules. We started to know that if running our offices had been up to us, we would probably have included some different criteria in our definition of business success. Women who have reached a level of achievement say that if they were *really* in charge, if things were *really* up to them, work would operate very differently. They would reward collaboration, not competition, among co-workers. They would share information and their definition of success would depend more on the quality of what was produced than on the system that produced it. Conventional business success, measured in power and hierarchy, would cede to job sharing and teamwork. As Anna Quindlen put it, "If women were in charge, we would feminize the way things work. Not just because we are right but because it would make things better for everyone."

But we aren't rewarded for working that way. And if we want our careers to continue to flourish, we start to find that how we act and what we privately feel are not always the same. We quickly learn that if we are to have any chance at competing for the good jobs, we go with what our office cultures dictate, even if it goes against our best interests. We find out that saying what we think and doing what we believe is right does not necessarily produce good results. If a woman wants to succeed, by the time she gets to her first job performance review, she has learned two things: 1) Her first job is the right behavior—right by what the prevailing culture says is right—and 2) if she wants to get ahead, acting right is more important than being right.

One of the greatest misconceptions I had when I began my career was that I would be judged and advanced by who I was as a person and by the quality of my work. Since I had done well in school, I assumed that the same standards would apply at work. I quickly discovered, however, that counterintuitive as it was, this was not going to be the case. I remember watching a young editor, Martha. She was a few years older than I. Her ability to transform even the dullest reference text into something glistening and enjoyable astounded me. She worked from eight A.M.

49

until well past eight P.M. every day, every night. She never complained (except to a few of us fellow underlings) and always gave her authors the credit for the masterly manuscript (or her supervising editor took it). Over the years she slowly crept up through the title brackets, never left the company for more money (indeed, because her bosses took most of the credit for her efforts, she remained virtually invisible to anyone who might have wanted to hire her), and lived in the same studio apartment paying for the rent increases with the commensurate measly merit increases she received annually. She was the stuff of which profitability is made, the glue that held seasonal publishing lists together, the overly responsible and utterly nonthreatening power behind the throne. She drew her identity from being needed and performing her work as perfectly as possible. She watched as other less talented young editors flashed by her to bigger offices, better titles, doubled salaries. At first she was mystified. "What are they doing that I'm not doing?" Then she grew judgmental. "Anyone can pay a ton of money to sign up a has-been movie star. My authors write real books." Finally, she was outraged. Her division, having been sold twice and reorganized once, was now going to be consolidated into a larger one and Martha was let go. "They can't imagine what's going to happen without me; they have no idea what goes on here. Good luck to them," she whistled in the dark. One of the new managers told me he was sorry to lose her because "she had the corporate memory." It would wound Martha deeply if she knew that, in the end, it was only her endurance that distinguished her, not her talents.

Being a good worker does not guarantee success. Loyalty,

dedication, excellence, and hard work without some form of self-promotion or some other way of being recognized often invites exile from the fast track. I have tried sitting back and hoping that someone will recognize my good work. In the culture of success this is seen as passivity—rarely an asset. Or, it's mistaken for a lack of fire, guts, or ambition.

Instead, only the classically ambitious way really works (although a woman shouldn't appear too strong or self-promoting—she is still supposed to be a "lady" and doesn't want to be accused of appearing tough or self-interested). Every woman entering the business world soon finds that, contrary to her academic experience, how well she performs actually is only one factor in creating a future for herself. Instead, an unwritten set of rules directs her fate—a Darwinian system that weeds out those with no stomach for politics, competition, or monofocused ambition. The rules of this system were designed to help men distinguish leaders from followers, and to determine who ran the pack as top dog. On a broader, less personal level these rules etch the form of a corporation or organization's culture. While each industry, company, or institution puts its own twist on them, all have a version of the rules and they govern the way each place of business works.

These rules aren't to be found in any employee handbook. If a person wants to succeed, however, it is important to follow the rules to the letter. Rule #1: Work comes first, above all personal or family concerns. Rule #1a: If you're a man and a father, you can break Rule #1 and be a great guy; if you're a woman and you break Rule #1, you're not serious about your future. That said, this rule works best with a little occasional sighing; after all, good women are supposed to want to be home with their kids. Rule #2: Long hours are a requirement. If your boss wants you and you're not there, he or she will learn quickly to want someone else who is. There is no Rule #2a; "face time" is an equal-opportunity requirement. Rule #3: Take credit for what works (no matter how tangential your role) and run from what doesn't. Rule #3a: If you're a man and you break Rule #3 because you gave credit to a woman, you immediately get more credit for yourself because of your fairness and magnanimity. If you are a woman and you think that Rule #3a behavior is disgusting, the resulting failure to follow Rule #3 results in perpetual middle management and the possibility that the words *good old* might eventually precede your name. On the other hand, too much exercise of this rule gets you the hard-to-lose epithet "aggressive"—and it's not a compliment. Rule #4: There is only one career in your life and only one path. If you step off it, you're out of luck. Rule #4a: If you are a man and you break Rule #4, you were probably downsized; tough luck, it won't hurt you. If you broke Rule #4 because you are a woman who stayed home with your children for a while, you are a swell person but a bad bet for future employment, to say nothing of advancement. Rule #5: This is about hierarchy. Your job is to make your boss look good and your boss's job is to make his or her boss look good. Rule #6: The goal is to get as close to the top as possible. There is no end to what you are supposed to achieve or want.

There is one final rule reserved for women: Work with the men, joke with the men. But never, ever, become one.

"At first I had to ask my husband to translate the rules for me," said Terry, a young attorney who was getting really poor cases to work on. "I honestly didn't understand what I was doing wrong. But now I just accept that if I keep quiet, I get the work I enjoy. I love what I do. I just accept that the environment surrounding it is all phony."

I ask Terry if she feels her approach has meant some personal compromises. "What do you mean?" she asks, puzzled. "I get to do the work I love, and they've even let me work four days a week since I had my son. It's hectic but I wouldn't want to give it up. No," she says after a pause, "I don't think I've paid a price."

But Ruth, another attorney who works with Terry, interrupts. "No price except the minute you went to a four-day week you were no longer in the running for partner or for any big job. Face it, Terry," Ruth states, "you're on the Mommy Track now."

I completely understand how Terry could mistake a penalty for a privilege. Infatuated with work, I was heavily invested in not seeing that simply being a woman carried potential consequences for my career; the question wasn't one of qualifications or ability, but simply that if I wanted to share in the real fruits of success, I either had to work as a man would work or face a career with more limited options and potential.

Failure to follow these rules not only meant a lifetime shunted off to a world where raises are measured in single-digit percentages. A lack of desire to play by them was interpreted as an inability to "cut it"—that a woman (or a man) didn't want "it" enough. Furthermore, something was clearly wrong if you didn't evidence a hungry ambition. If you stopped trying to move forward, you were passed over. Fighting the idea of sufficiency, ignoring the validity of contentment, the only time these rules let people accept what they had was when it became very clear that there were no more mountains to scale in their future.

A Double Standard of Success

These rules for fitting in and succeeding are not just guidelines for success but the bones of a value system—the one that governed our fathers' lives. When we adopt the conventional picture of success, we are forced to live by its values. These values ask us to judge ourselves by our behavior, by our outsides and accomplishments. We become valued by what we do, not by who we are.

This success value system has a subtle and extremely corrosive part to it: It's all or nothing. It equates self-sacrifice with success. In order to achieve, the men who designed the rules had to give themselves over to their careers. They had to abandon their homes and families for hours and days at a time. Because achievement was society's most important measure of a person's worth, this system makes no allowance for anything to be more important than work.

This causes a problem for women because we have another requirement for success that society expects from us and that we expect from ourselves. From the beginning we are told (explicitly or by example) that our success will be measured not only by our work but by our ability to be "women." That means, for most of us, by the kind of man we attract and family we do or don't produce. Even if we don't want to get married and have children,

54

the expectation still lurks in the corner and can make us feel as though we are failing. Gloria Steinem put it this way: "If you meet a woman who's doing wonderfully well professionally, doing great, creative things, and is completely happy with her work but she doesn't have the personal life she thinks she's supposed to have, she may think she's a failure. Men are the reverse. They can have great personal lives, and think they're failures if they don't have the job success they think they are supposed to have."

These two different qualifications for success can create a crisis for women. We don't want to fully embrace a value system that asks us to sacrifice ourselves on the altar of success. We value our home lives and even if we didn't we're still primarily responsible for them. It's also difficult—at best—to adopt a system which assigns to that traditional "women's work" a lesser value than work in the office if it accords it any value at all. So, we go to work as outsiders. Warren Farrell, author of *Why Men Are the Way They Are,* observes that "women don't ever completely take on this male value system." After observing the differences in the way women and men value success, he says that "a working woman today has grown up with two value systems: the system of her mother, which said be nurturing, be a mother. And the other was the value system of her father from which she can either deviate or imitate."

Deviation, imitation. One doesn't get us very far, but the other asks us to split ourselves into two. Internally this choice sets up a kind of slow-release schizophrenia. Women want to hold on to what makes them women while simultaneously recognizing that many of those qualities are going to make them outsiders in the male work culture. This dynamic starts to pull us apart. We didn't see this in the beginning of our careers because we were being well and rapidly rewarded. Most of us didn't have husbands or home lives to distract us from our immediate professional challenges. We were our jobs and our jobs created the good things in our lives.[1]

But when we start to have demands outside of work, we begin to see that the cost of success can be a very divided life. We still expect that we should be able to do it all, but we are beginning to experience that the structures and demands of our work make no room for our personal lives. Yet, as women, not only do we want husbands and families, we know we will be judged as incomplete women by society if we don't have them. When these opposing pressures, these opposing value systems, start to fight each other, we start to see that meeting our great expectations for our lives is going to be a lot of work.

Every woman I interviewed had elements of this double standard but none more than Cindy Mason, a forty-two-year-old political consultant in Washington. Cindy says that she knows she has two definitions for a successful life, but she is still unable to get a handle on which one rules. She is unable to integrate them into one place. She talks quickly as we sit in her open, sun-streaked living room, delighted, she says, to find that she isn't the only one who feels completely nuts on this topic. "There is the 'private' me," she explains, "which is much more sensual. It's traveling, cooking, listening to music, reading. It's experiences, how things feel. The work person is frantic. Absorption, complete immersion in one thing and being obsessed with it and thinking about it every minute and thinking about everything that could go wrong, anticipating everything. It's like a little timer goes off and all of a sudden I get completely focused. It's exhausting and there's no room for anything else. I can't seem to let the sensual things come in; they'll distract me. So I can't integrate my lives. I really can't. That would be ideal, but what I do is go into the happiness side for a while and then the obsessive side for a while. I haven't seen a model of what I would consider serious work identity that doesn't pull me into this obsessing."

Partly due to the nature of her work and completely due to the nature of her character, Cindy has boomeranged back and forth between two models: flat-out work and being a wife and mother. Yet she can never stay at home too long; too many messages intrude. "Some of the aspects of feminism I internalized said that it's bad to be dependent on someone else, a man, and that homemaker things are not as valuable and that you don't deserve anything unless you're working. Work is what makes you a person." She continued, "I heard, 'Women can do anything men can do,' which is true. But the next thing is that they *should* do it. And if they don't, they are not as valuable a person as those who are. It's not just that you can do everything, it's that you've got to prove it by doing it."

The dynamic between Cindy's parents accounts for some of her inability to integrate her whole self into her work. "My recollection of my mother is that she always felt inferior." Cindy recalls that her mother's silent protest was *I didn't go to college, I'm just a housewife,* and Cindy picked that up. "In my house it wasn't 'Oh, your mother is perfect and wonderful.' She was. She was an incredibly wonderful and nurturing mom. She was always there and there was always dinner. But my dad said to us, 'You shouldn't just have your mother's life.' And the more he encouraged us, the more upset she got because he was putting her down. But I identify with my mother in a lot of ways. I like to make everything nice and comfortable. They are part of my values. They aren't boys' values. The girl was supposed to have both sets of values, which is very hard.

"My father projected what was important in life and what he said was the center of everything. Everything revolved around his career, his tastes. He did send very mixed signals. Yes, it was important to have a career, but he was in a glamour business so he also told us it was also important to be attractive like the actresses and quiet like my mother."

Cindy has spent her remarkable political career rocketing between the two role extremes. A Stanford Law School graduate, Cindy fell into politics as a behind-the-scenes expert and has worked in Washington and Texas for twenty years. Those years have been punctuated, however, by four or five "sabbaticals"—or rather attempts at them. The first came after her stint as a chief of staff for a state legislator. It was a draining experience, fun, but exhausting. After a while she was miserable from overwork and the internal political dynamics. "So, I quit. I'm twenty-eight, I'm a kid. I'm young, I thought, *I'm going to garden, run, get in shape.* So, I started running. I ran and ran and ran and ran. I got up to eight miles a day and I was hysterical. Absolutely hysterical. *Everyone is going to forget about you,* I thought, and *You're never going to get a job and you're not earning any money. It's completely unacceptable and people are going to think you're crazy.* So I just couldn't take the sabbatical. I lasted six months; it was supposed to be a year but I just couldn't do it."

When Cindy married and had a son, her internal drama escalated. "You are identified by who you are and you've got to have a job," she says. "Work was my identity and that was where I felt competent. I felt completely incompetent with an infant." One of the silent casualties in the process of achieving success has been the value we assign to the traditional and unremunerated tasks of friendship, partnering, and motherhood. That was certainly Cindy's feeling. Anything that smacked of her mother's life felt like failure. Where her mother devoted her life to her husband and kids, Cindy couldn't wait to get back to work after the birth of her child. The baby was very delicate and Cindy felt unsure about taking care of him. "I couldn't get back to work fast enough. I stayed out ten weeks and I never stayed home with him. I feel terrible about that now. It was a terrible mistake." Cindy tried three more times over the years to stay home or work part-time; she felt she was falling down on the mother side of life. But it never lasted more than six months. Cindy acknowledges that her approach to answering both parts of herself has luxury elements to it; she has a husband who has a job. Even so, she feels completely worthless if she isn't earning money. "None of my value systems go together," Cindy concludes, sighing. "It's really hard."

Cindy rejected her mother's role completely. She saw how devalued her mother's life was in both her parents' eyes. Yet, not surprisingly, her nonwork self—what she called her sensual self— contains many of what she feels were her mother's defining character traits. Cindy cannot incorporate this part of herself into her life because she saw these things so completely dismissed in her household growing up. Instead of being able to open her defini-

59

tion of success to include facets of what she loves about being a mother, she trundles back and forth between the opposite poles of the workaholic and the total mom. Ironically, the parts of her that she didn't value actually interfered with her career, because she learned from her mother that to be appreciated you don't "toot your own horn, you don't organize people to call the mayor on your behalf, and you just sit there and expect everyone to appreciate you." As a consequence, she says, she became "self-deprecating, self-sabotaging, self-vetting. It's pretend, because you do think you are good enough to be all these things, but you think that it is not becoming to go for them." Cindy's selves jockey for position, costing her any true satisfaction with where she is or what she is doing at any given time. Sadly, they also cost Cindy her fantasy career working with child welfare issues; "It's ironic," she concludes as she looks out her window, "that I was so determined to have a work identity, it actually got in the way of what I really wanted to do. It was more important for me to prove I could be successful in the short term than to pursue a long-term dream."

Cindy happened to get the message about what was valued and what wasn't from watching her parents. She could have received it from television, school, church or synagogue, friends, magazines, newspapers, radio, or her favorite clothing store. The message was simple: If a young woman wanted to be successful in her own eyes as well as in society's, her accomplishments had to look a whole lot like her father's.

Yet her home life had to look a whole lot like her mother's.

Expectations and Success

In a delayed reaction to the mixed signals she received about what is important in life, Cindy has found herself in a state of semiparalysis. She can't figure out which definition of success feels more comfortable for her. She knows she will never be a stay-at-home mom, but having repeatedly tried the workaholic life, she knows the answer doesn't lie there either. Cindy can't untangle the knot of messages she has inside about who she's supposed to be and what's going to make her happy. She is carrying on what is fast becoming a tradition of confusion. In 1976, when Cindy was graduating from law school, there were ads that told her she could "bring home the bacon and fry it up in a pan." In 1996, the ads still carry an unrealistic message. One designer two-page spread shows a picture of a beautiful, thin, almost forty-something woman out for a run, pushing a baby in a baby jogger. The headline asks, WHO SAYS THIS WOMAN ISN'T WORKING? Who do they think they're kidding?

These new images of success show a casual, almost effortless, combination of roles. This fantasy not only contradicts women's direct experience but it simultaneously reinforces a feeling of inadequacy. Many have tried these approaches and found instead that they have paid a professional price. We have attempted different solutions applied in Band-Aid form that may have temporarily turned down the heat on the boiling-over pot of our lives, but the problems underneath didn't disappear. We wonder what we are doing wrong—as if our inability to find happiness lies in a failure of will or effort or smarts on our part. When we pick apart the individual pieces of our lives, we see we have done pretty well.

61

Yet the sum of the parts hasn't added up to a whole. The messages from one world are frustrated by the messages from the other. This isn't what success was supposed to feel like.

The clash of messages that existed between Cindy's parents now has moved between her ears. But she doesn't feel she can enjoy either role. Every decision and every action in one world seems to take away from the other. She's supposed to be hard-working, but not self-promoting, she's supposed to work like a man but act like a woman. She's supposed to do her job with total dedication but make her home the center of her life. She's supposed to be in the center of her world but keep to the sidelines as a support for her husband and family. The more demanding her career, the less time she has for herself, her home, her friends, her family. The more focus on her personal life, the more risk she runs of not being taken seriously at work.

Like Cindy we keep turning the knobs—a little more here, a little less there—in an effort to get the inner and outer balances correct. Of course, this is impossible because no one can do it all. But we still expect it. At this point in our lives most of us define ourselves through our careers. But we are beginning to see that balance will elude us as long as we identify ourselves according to two different pictures of who we're supposed to be. We are beginning to see that there is a price for this work-based identity, a price for success that we pay for with our lives.

CHAPTER 3

The Price of Success

T HE KIND OF SUCCESS E LLIE ENJOYED
works best if you are a woman without a home life working in an
expanding economy. But in the mid-1980s Wall Street, like the
rest of the business world, took a serious downward turn. Even in
the face of rising stock values and corporate profits, businesses
began a decade-long infatuation with reengineering and downsizing. Almost overnight it seemed that the corporate world con-
tracted. Middle managers became endangered species. Everyone
found they were working longer, harder, and for fewer rewards.
As for Ellie, her area of expertise—public finance—was deci-
mated. And in the new climate of scarcity her work world quickly
became divided into two very distinct teams: The Good Old Boys
and the Also-Rans—a motley combination of women and nerds.
Ellie officially joined the latter camp when she walked into the
office one day to find her division dissolved and her new supervisor a man who had been her peer the day before. "As bad as that
was," Ellie recalls, "I still hung in there. I thought I needed the

63

dough. And I certainly needed the affirmation. Probably not in that order. But a tiny crack in the dream started for me that day. For the first time I started to see that work wasn't going to be 'the answer.'"

This reversal gave Ellie a chance to get some perspective on her life. When the outward rewards slipped away, she started to see that she didn't have much else in her life besides work and that her personal life hadn't fallen into place as expected. "I started to see how much the job was taking out of my soul. I was struggling to fit my life in around the crumbs of time that were left out of my job. That's what I did for fifteen years: fit in a little life here, cram in a dinner there. The job was the big picture and I just fit in these little snippets of having a life. I always thought that if I just had control of my job, everything else would happen. I just had to get to work so I could kill myself and I'd get the money to buy the things. I thought, *One day I'll be struck married and one day I will be struck with a life.* I don't know how I thought that would happen, but I knew it would somehow." But it didn't. At least not in time to have a family.

Ellie feels a bit ambivalent about that part, though. In the middle of our second interview my son streaked though the living room holding his diaper in his hands like a bagged bird; I could see her relief when he sped out just as quickly. "I just wonder if I really had it in me," she says. "I feel like I *should* have wanted kids, but if you want to know the honest truth, I like my privacy, I like my free time, I like having control over my life." But Ellie isn't so sanguine about not having a mate. "I just never put it on the priority list. Instead, I took the easy way out. I don't think I've had a boyfriend in the same time zone, no less city, in the past ten years. It's easy to stay together that way, but impossible for a relationship to go beyond a certain point."

Ellie feels the road is quickly narrowing in her life. Faced with the consequences of decisions she made (or didn't make) earlier in her life, she now recognizes the nature of the trade-offs involved in her career for her success. "The job was okay. I asked too much of it, but that's my particular set of baggage. Instead of looking to a man, I looked to my work for love and approval, recognition and attention. Which, for a long time, I got. But in the end the joke was on me. Because my work wasn't even what I thought it was. One day I saw the bonus grid in my boss's office. Right on the other side of my box the guys above me were making a fortune. I saw that they were only stringing along the appropriate number of females to keep the field diverse. It wasn't that I was valuable or important to the team. They had been blowing smoke in my face. The guy I reported to knew I was getting screwed and that he was being overpaid. But he knows that if he keeps his mouth shut, he keeps getting paid. The rewards for kissing ass and keeping the charade going were clear. It was the defining moment for me." Ellie realized that she had been keeping her relationship with work going—even in the face of diminishing returns—by selling her life at a discount. Because she had no life other than work, she couldn't look at the problem—there was nowhere else for her to go. We've all stayed in relationships longer than we knew we should because we were afraid of being alone, and this was true of Ellie and her job. But when she could no longer deny the price she was paying, the game was exposed. Ellie finally allowed herself to see what she wouldn't look at before. "It was time to get a life. I thought that work was life. How wrong that was for me."

Like Ellie, for a long time I was afraid to look at my relationship with my work. Deep down, I suspect I knew intuitively that my increasing disaffection couldn't be written off exclusively to the problems of the male/female dynamic—sexism, the glass ceiling, the old boy networks, women's continued disproportionate responsibility for home as well as office. Certainly those oft-discussed and very well documented realities accounted for an enormous part of my frustration and exhaustion. But there was another less obvious contributor. One that I wasn't aware of until work stopped being everything to me. One that, like most women, I would have denied if you told me about it. One that women don't discuss because it's painful to see and even harder to admit. It's part of the price we pay for success and it happens in subtle and tiny increments. It's disguised even to us as "getting along" or "fitting in." It isn't unlike what happens to young girls when they enter adolescence as they discover that being accepted by the guys means making sure they don't appear too smart, too strong, or too different. Too threatening. Instead, we bury ourselves with silence, giving up who we are in exchange for having our careers.

This curious thing happened on the way to the office. Rather than changing the culture we entered, we seem, instead, to have accommodated it. Or, we just resigned ourselves to it. And this separates us from ourselves. At first this division seems like simple dues paying. As one accountant said, "What choice is there? You can't change it. You're either a player or you aren't. If you want to be one, you have to play the game on their terms." We are willing to change our outward behaviors to get a chance at the interesting assignments and to have an equal shot at the rewards and privileges of work, and inside, we know we aren't the person we sometimes pretend to be. But this double life takes a slow toll on us. We start to resent our work for asking us to dissemble and we start to lose self-esteem for doing so. Of course, there are women (and we can all probably quickly name one or two in our lives) who didn't have to do that. Most of us, however, face a simple choice—we either fit in or we don't get very far.

It's not that I was a macho female from nine to five and a real femme from five to nine. I was more or less the same, somewhat outspoken, opinionated woman at work and at home. Like many of the successful women I interviewed, I considered myself a feminist and felt I had an obligation to speak out and not hide my light under my business suit. But as time went on, as I became responsible for more than myself, that more gutsy, abrasive side quieted down. I often found myself faced with the option of being what I considered "right" or getting the resources I needed to do the job correctly. I could either make a stand, or save the energy, keep the confidence of the person who hired me, and be able to publish a book well or hire another person. In my quest to have it all I put away part of myself.

I remember my first mentor (who actually ended up leaving our company for moral reasons) advising me to "pick my battles." Over time it became increasingly clear that the people who nodded in meetings, performed without question the (sometimes pointless) tasks assigned, and then went about their business retained the respect of their supervisors and were rewarded with better jobs. "You have to learn to manage up," I was advised by someone who worked for me. "You'll throw it all away if you don't." I knew she was right. I hated doing it. But I had begun to see that the ends justified the means.

Progressively, then, I found myself making the same accommodations I saw being made by the pioneering women ahead of me. But they *had* to adapt. They were necessarily focused on the *right* to work, not transforming its values. "When I started out, I had to be a different person at the office," says Edith, a sixty-six-year-old retired magazine publisher. "I was the only woman in a three-martini world. Don't look at my behavior without looking at the times," she cautions. "My battle was to *get* there and *stay* there. Not to *change* there." Women like Edith had no choice but to split themselves apart: to fit in at work they had to join the culture already under way—one that was profoundly male, dedicated to self-definition by occupation. As Rosabeth Moss Kanter points out, "It was rarity and scarcity, rather than femaleness per se, that shaped the environment for women. The life of women in the corporation was influenced by the proportions in which they found themselves. Those women who were few in number among male peers and often had 'only woman' status became tokens. . . . Sometimes they had the advantages of those who are 'different' and thus highly visible in a system where success is tied to becoming known. Sometimes they faced the loneliness of the outsider, of the stranger who intrudes upon an alien culture and may become self-estranged in the process of assimilation."[1]

When my peers and I entered the business world, we found a world with its rules still largely unaltered by the presence of women. The agenda of success came first. We learned that if we really wanted the chance to do meaningful work, if we really wanted the opportunity to succeed, we had to make some serious adjustments in our priorities. We had to work as the men worked. We are all too aware of the inner and outer consequences if we don't. As Barbara Sher, best-selling author and career counselor, points out, "Even a woman who has raised children with support and understanding will apply the 'male military standard' to herself and feel like a failure when she comes up short. We're all taught that real winners can take abuse. Such yardsticks exist in our culture and we're trained to measure ourselves against them no matter how little they apply to us. It's a funny thing: when the shoe doesn't fit we think we're supposed to wear it anyway." The necessary result of all this is profound stress. Women work under a no-win paradox: We need our work to be fully realized as women but in order to do the work we have to silence a good deal of ourselves.

Denial

The way most of us deal with this self-defeating conflict is to deny it exists and that we are participating in it. When I switched to the editorial side of the publishing business, which was filled with women, I thought, *Great! Now I can be myself.* But when I got there I found a culture similar to the more male world of sales and marketing. At first I was mildly surprised but I quickly got used to it. What other example did I have? Because it's too painful to see what we trade for success, we instead enter into a weird state of denial. It tells us that we actually don't mind things the way they are. After all, we love our jobs and the rest is just the price of admission. This denial tells us we are being judged by our abilities and our ambition and our sex is not a real handicap. It tells us that we can have our jobs and our homes, that we can have it all without a penalty other than running out of time in our day. It promises we can fake it—we can take on values of the hero system without it really affecting us. Actually, it tells us we *want* to embrace those values because they make us successful. Thanks to the cultural backlash against feminism, it tells us that we aren't "those" kind of strident women who are so hard to get along with; we are the kind of women with whom men are glad to share their offices. To back this up we point out how we were sponsored by male mentors, promoted by male superiors. We blend into the culture, identify our goals by what those above us on the corporate ladder have. We are satisfied with our progress and we think that the world has no more discrimination. By 1996, 54 percent of the self-identified professional women in my survey said that the women's movement had no effect on their lives whatsoever. Putting aside the fact that less than 2 percent of women in the United States have penetrated the upper executive ranks,[2] they might be more right than they know. In terms of the corporate culture, that is.

I intimately understand this denial. As a product of a once all-male college I prided myself on the fact that I was able to slip into a male world and be accepted. And because I saw this as undeniable progress for women and because I was enjoying the privileges of the system, I didn't see that I had slowly come to identify with a value system that ultimately wasn't going to recognize all of me or serve my interests. But in the early days I was also single and childless and young, and I was being nicely rewarded

70

with money and power and position. There was, as yet, no point where my professional and personal interests differed. I couldn't see that I had a time bomb of dual identities ticking away inside me. I couldn't see that living with the values of the hero system would slowly create a distance between my professional and personal selves. I didn't see it, that is, until I was very far down the road.

I developed what Rosabeth Moss Kanter observed in many women in corporations; she called it "a public persona that hid inner feelings."[3] I became the title on my business card. And while it was never a totally comfortable fit, I gauged it to be an essential part of my wardrobe, like panty hose or a briefcase. Most of us know how this public face works. On the simplest surface level it's the "up" smile we put on during the five minutes of joking around before the weekly operations meeting. It's the one that doesn't openly protest the Saturday strategic planning meeting when we know that's our precious time with our kids. It's the incredibly responsible person who smiles and says, "Sure, no problem," to extra work that will mean staying late. It's the perfectionist who knocks herself out to do flawless work and then pretends it was nothing. Each woman interviewed remembered times when she kept silent, obeyed a directive that she knew was a total waste of time and energy, didn't ask for a salary increase when it was due or take time off because she feared the consequences on her career. Our spirits are eroded by maintaining silence in the face of politics and backstabbing, by living in a crisis and pressure mentality all the time. It has little to do with performing good work or being productive and everything to do with pecking orders and egos. Finally, having spent years paying our dues in this culture, we become so identified with it that we come to believe in its rules and we pass the system along to the next generation of women. As our careers advance on these terms, a piece of ourselves retreats.

Over time this public face proves to be more than an effective tool for fitting in; it becomes our work identity. On a profound level this identity forces us to compartmentalize our lives. We know there are parts of us—parts that we love—that, if shown at the office, make us seem less effective, less valuable, or diminish our chances at work we really want. I knew a woman, Toni, who was seen as an "emotional" person at her office. But she was a creative director, so people "made allowances" for her behavior— creative people were allowed to be volatile. To a point, that is. When Toni went through an unwanted divorce, she found it impossible to segregate her mourning to the off hours. Sensitive to the fact that her office didn't easily accept "female" behavior, she took time off or tried to cry in her office with the door shut. After a few weeks her supervisor told her she had to pull it together. She tried, and actually got back on track. But when her division was asked to downsize a few months later, Toni found herself with a pink slip after ten years. She felt that "it was because I couldn't pretend nothing had happened to me. My boss's boss had gone through this big intracompany love affair that everyone knew about and he wasn't fired, because he just went on as if nothing had happened. I have no doubts that if I could have been an automaton I would be employed today." Through observation and intuition we learn that aspects of who we are as women have no place in the office. Instead, they live in their own personal world, shoved to the edges of the day, left at home next to the newspaper and the half-drunk cup of coffee waiting for our return from work.

Just One of the Guys

I spent most of my career in traditionally male jobs—first sales and marketing and then management—and I often found myself in positions where there were few other women around. While to my knowledge I never became more stereotypically "manly" than the men around me, I nevertheless knew how to emphasize those parts of my character that made it easier for me to fit in with the guys. It looked like I really enjoyed competing; I developed sarcastic humor. When I was unlucky enough to have an enormous account return more books that it had ordered one month (thus causing the first negative sales in the company's history) I didn't duck into the office of the guy next door to talk about how scared I was I would lose my job. He was more of a competitor than a commiserater. Instead, I smiled in outward good humor, as I became the butt of most of the jokes around the sales floor until some other poor jerk took my place at the bottom of the food chain. I traveled with the guys as sexlessly as possible, hung out at the bars with them, and ignored any sodden, suggestive remarks that sometimes floated across sales conference cocktail tables late at night after a few too many. I knew enough not to take visible offense at jokes that involved female body parts lest I be labeled a woman "who couldn't take a joke." I even looked the other way when, a few years later, one of my bosses asked, in a drunken moment, if he "couldn't kiss that spot between my eyebrows."

(That was after I refused to go to his room for "a meeting" just between the two of us.) For my compliance there were rewards. I felt included and I loved being affectionately introduced as "one of the guys." I bent over backward to fit in; true, I wanted to succeed, but I also wanted to be liked and accepted. I loved my work, I was having a ball, and I never really gave my behavior a second thought.

One of the most disturbing forms of this denial comes when women, for the sake of advancement or job security, actually turn against other women's interests. One woman told of a time when she was working in a small division of a large media company, seven women out of a staff of forty-eight were pregnant at the same time. Trying to avoid a problem, a group of employees asked the division head (a man with children whose wife had stopped working) to see if they could work out flexible schedules, create job sharing, and, for those whose work was self-contained, four-day weeks. The company was highly sophisticated technologically; these women could work from home one day a week. Some were willing to forgo a fifth of their salaries as it would be cheaper than child care, which would have freed enough money to hire another person on a job-sharing basis. When he said that selectively changing the five-day-a-week schedule would set a precedent that could lead to chaos and ill will toward the mothers, the women appealed to his number two to support the cause—after all, she had two young daughters and shared the same pressures. But she simply said, "It's too much work to juggle all that, it has never been done here and would set a bad precedent. It wouldn't be good for morale," she continued. "What about the people with no children? Besides," she said, "we weren't having a good enough year that we were in any kind of bargaining position." The women pointed out that other people might also want to take advantage of increased flexibility or for their own personal reasons. But the business manager said that the women would have to figure it out for themselves—that unfortunately, that's just the way it was there. The division head is still there. The number two is still there. Only one of the seven women is left.

The saddest part of the story is that this woman did not want to make any other woman's life more difficult. She was apparently a nice person who sincerely wanted the best for everyone. But her concept of that was a division which functioned with full-time on-site employees. She genuinely believed she was making a good business decision. But over the years she had had to make so many personal trades in her own life that she stopped questioning whether or not those trades were necessary. Frankly, it was probably too difficult emotionally for her to open up the issue and see where constructive changes could transform and improve a very rigid (and increasingly unhappy and unprofitable) work environment.

A less stark example was Jennifer, a marketing director for a financial services company. When I interviewed a few women who worked with and for her, they all said they respected her, admired her, even, for her professionalism and dedication. But after a while, a deeper, more mistrustful feeling came out. "You never really know what she's thinking," one woman said. "But you can be sure she'll toe the party line."

When the company had a change in management, Jennifer quickly became the new president's favorite person. "He was one of these McKinsey consultant types," another woman recalled.

"He knew next to nothing about what we do but Jennifer became his teacher and his Stepin Fetchit. You'd never catch her saying a bad thing about him or anything at all, and it became hard to trust her after a while; she was just an extension of him." Jennifer was promoted shortly after the new president's arrival. According to her co-workers, she had become the kind of woman in business that author Susan Wittig Albert describes beautifully in her book *Work of Her Own:*

> We easily recognize a woman at the pinnacle of her career. She is a self-realized, self-determined, stand-alone person. She has an autonomous, independent identity, the major components of which include her work, her title, and the status and prestige that come with the titles—all conferred by the work institution to which she belongs. She has successfully climbed the masculine staircase of adult growth and development. . . . As she moves up the work world, the successful woman is required to repudiate most of what makes her a woman: her feminine viewpoint, her feminine values of nurturing and caring. In order to succeed she develops a strongly male-oriented bias and a tendency to uphold and defend the masculine culture of ideas and ideals. . . .[4]

Rosabeth Moss Kanter points out that the behavior of women like Jennifer or the business manager is the result of very deeply embedded forces. By allying themselves with those in power they receive "an instant identity"[5] but at the same time become "psychological hostages to the majority group. . . . The price of being 'one of the boys' was a willingness to occasionally turn against 'the girls.' "[6] Many women told me versions of this story. "If someone had a life, it became submerged by the female version of macho," said Nancy Bramwell, a vice president at a manufacturing firm. "Some women became antifeminist as a way to be a part of the good-old-boy network. These were women with children. But they saw that in order to be in with the 'in' crowd, female issues weren't to be discussed. When I adopted two children at the same time, instead of cutting me some flexibility, the attitude from both men and women was 'This is your personal problem. Go fix it.' That is not what the woman's movement was about. It became co-opted and twisted."

She's right, of course. But we don't address our daily lives in such a philosophical fashion. For us it's more a matter of going to work, doing what we can to feel secure, accepted, or appreciated. I know of no woman who consciously sets out to silence a part of herself. But I know of many who feel it's more important to be securely in the boat than to rock it. Underneath that decision lies the complex and painful web of self-denial.

Trained to Fit In

I clearly remember the moment I switched from my compass to Mrs. Ryan's. I was in seventh grade and had just moved to New York from a small town in Connecticut. The girls seemed so sophisticated, so poised. I wore orthopedic shoes and had rubber bands in my braces. Fitting in socially mattered to me; I didn't want to be a geek. Instead, Mrs. Ryan completely turned me around that first day of school when she announced that everything we would be doing would be in preparation for getting into a good college: It was going to be either/or. Social acceptance or never getting into college. Ultimately, I went to college. I made only one friend in high school.

In *Mother Daughter Revolution* authors Marie Wilson, Idelisse Malavé, and Elizabeth Debold point out that women learn early on that to fit in to the dominant culture they have to "give up parts of themselves to be safe and accepted within society. Once [there], it becomes hard to recognize its structure as anything but 'reality.' " Their book, like Carol Gilligan's *In a Different Voice* or Mary Pipher's *Reviving Ophelia,* document in stunning terms what happens to girls as they enter the male culture somewhere around adolescence. "With puberty girls face enormous cultural pressure to split into false selves," says Pipher. "Girls can be true to themselves and risk abandonment by their peers, or they can choose their true selves and be socially acceptable. Most girls choose to be socially accepted and split into two selves, one that is authentic and one that is culturally scripted. In public they become who they are supposed to be."[7] Girls are asked to not be too smart, too aggressive, too individual, too masculine. "Adolescent girls discover that it is impossible to be both feminine and adult," says Pipher, pointing to the famous study by psychologist I. K. Broverman. That study, which asked men and women to describe the traits of healthy men, healthy women, and healthy adults, documented that people of both sexes described healthy men and healthy adults in the same terms. Healthy women, however, had different qualities. They were expected to be passive, dependent, and emotional. But as Pipher points out, that knowledge alone means little: "The rules for girls are confusing and the deck is stacked against them, but they soon learn that this is the only game in town."

As we talk about this, Idelisse Malavé, former vice president for the Ms. Foundation and currently head of the Tides Foundation, throws up her hands. "I'm a feminist!" she exclaims. "I have a twelve-year-old daughter who goes to an all-girl school. She has many adult women role models in her life. And she is bombarded with alternatives to the girls-will-be-boys way of life. Yet, when she thinks of herself as the best, it's when she's being one of the guys." Malavé points out that far from being an adolescent problem, most studies show that the more young women become immersed in school and college, the more their minds develop, the more they experience the true nature of what women's place is in the world, the more it impacts on their dreams and aspirations.[8] "As a matter of fact," she says with a laugh, "if you didn't respond that way, something would be wrong with you. There's one researcher in Canada whom I have always adored for saying that if girls' self-esteem didn't drop at the edge of adolescence and continue dropping as they got older, they'd be crazy!"

We're not crazy, though, not in the way Malavé means. We silence ourselves because it offers us very real benefits. Sometimes we call the silence dues. Sometimes we even have the presence of mind to know that if we give a little, we get a lot.

The Consequences

Harvard Project member and author Elizabeth Debold has been researching and observing this self-defeating pattern in young girls and women for years. "What naturally happens when you overlay yourself and develop a false self that goes against core values and connections is depression. This is a totally predictable result because what you are doing is dampening, silencing, and subduing a whole part of who you are." What happens, Debold says, is that over time the rage at having to trade in whole parts of ourselves builds up so much that it could blow up the world. "The submerged parts of yourself that you roped into a really fragile balance start to move around. We get furious at our bosses, our co-workers, our mates, our children. We start to feel that at any time the lid might blow sky high. But we keep saying, 'Things are fine, the problem's just me,' because to engage in the bigger problem, the institutionalized problem, is too overwhelming, too enraging. Women don't yet have a decent way of analyzing this and the working world hasn't changed enough so that there are any real alternatives."

"I will never forget the morning I woke up and announced to my husband that I'd finally gone insane," Stephanie Rosen, a thirty-nine-year-old attorney, recalled. "I'd just woken from one of those anxiety dreams, the ones where someone you love is about to die and you feel like you are running through Jell-O to try and reach them, which of course, you never do. I realized then that the person I was trying to save was me." Stephanie had just come off a three-year case only to find out she wasn't going to be made partner in her law firm. "Part of it was exhaustion, part of it was anger at having knocked myself out for all those years, and for what?" But the part that really got to her was that as humiliated as she felt by not being accepted to the insider's level, she was stuck. Her husband had started a psychotherapy practice after years of training, but it couldn't pay their bills. And worse, there was nothing else she could think of that she wanted to do. It wasn't just the car payments, it was the fact that she relied on her job for a feeling she was worth something in this world. "I went into this deep depression. Nothing mattered. I couldn't get out of bed. I gained about fifteen pounds overnight," she recalled. "I've never felt so trapped in all my life." Clinical psychotherapist Lynne Hennecke, Ph.D., defines this kind of depression as "anger at someone or something you think you need. Since it feels like you need that person or job, it feels dangerous to get angry, which leads to a feeling of real helplessness. If this goes on long enough, you start to feel hopeless and trapped." Because our jobs are so important to who we are, we can't afford to put them in jeopardy, psychologically or physically. How ironic to feel trapped by the very thing we thought would set us free.

Elizabeth Debold points out that if the depression can turn into anger, good things can come of it. "The woman's movement was founded on rage," she notes. "The question is how do you take that rage, that energy, that sense of 'I can't believe this!' and use it? If you can't use it," she concludes, "it feels like it will just corrode your insides."

Corrosion or exhaustion. Exhaustion or depression. Depression or overeating. Overeating or drinking too much. Drinking too much or spending too much. The ways we fill the gap between who we really are and the ways we feel we must behave to advance in our careers are uncountable.

81

Oh, My God! I Forgot to Get Married!

One of the most painful consequences of denial has to do with the clock. Because we are working in a system designed for men, our career paths are linear and hierarchical. Men don't really have to adjust to the more circular rhythms and demands of families: for the most part they still have wives to manage the demands of raising children or caring for aging parents. Men work in a straight line, and to keep work satisfying and gratifying, the higher they go, the more interesting their work lives become, and the better they are rewarded.

Understandably, women want these same privileges. But to get them we have to delay marriage and children until we feel more secure about our careers. We simply don't have the option of dropping out or cutting back for a while. We know how hard it is to compete with men, or with women without families, on four hours of sleep or with a sick kid at home. So what many women do is wait. We wait to have families until we feel we have some job security and until we feel our accomplishments are beyond question. And women who wait sometimes find it isn't so easy after a certain point. When I had my son, I was thirty-eight. My doctor and the hospital treated me like the elderly primate that I was statistically. But I was lucky; unlike some of my friends I'd had no problems conceiving. The National Center for Health Statistics reports that roughly a quarter of all first-time births are to women aged thirty to forty-four, which is more than double the percentage of thirty years ago. No matter what the exact statistics or the exact age, it is irrefutable that decreasing fertility and "impaired fecundity" are a fact of life from sometime in the early thirties on. Jean Beward, a social worker in California, said, "People's life trajectories are very complicated, and circumstances are not always within our control. Knowing the facts may not have an impact on a woman's behavior, but I think it's valuable for women to have the information so that they can make informed choices."[9]

With such important issues at stake the pressure increases, and the gap between what is best for our business lives and what we want for our personal ones widens. The system of career advancement was not designed with biological clocks in mind. The average age for partnership decision in a law firm is thirty-four and in an accounting firm about the same. Stock options and profit sharing usually don't become part of a compensation package until an employee reaches director level. After working for ten to twelve years women are understandably reluctant to jeopardize the rewards. When the question of whether or not to have a child pits us against ourselves, many of us get understandably resentful.

For women who have children, there are consequences. Nancy remembers running into a woman she had once worked with. The woman had worked part-time for a while and then left. Nancy asked her how hard it had been to quit. "Leaving was easy," the woman said. "When I went part-time, that was the tough moment. That's when I sent out the message: I was stepping off the treadmill. I was telling people that work was no longer the most important thing to me. I took myself out of the promotion track and almost immediately got cut out of decisions. That was the hardest thing. It's as if all my experience was useless overnight. Going to full-time mom was easy after that."

Because many women suspect the grave truth about that woman's experience, many redouble their efforts to show that family will not have an effect on their work. They live in one of the most painful states of denial of all. Sandra Brass recently adopted a baby: "At work, sometimes I find no difference at all and at other times I feel like I'm not giving as much. In fact, I'm not, because the truth is that I'm exhausted. What is really suffering is the work outside of work. I'm not rushing home and working; I'm rushing home and seeing my baby. I thought I'd work on the train. I'd work smarter. It's not getting done. Now I work late one night a week. And I have tried hard not to let it show. If I get invited out in the evening, I am right there Johnny-on-the-spot. I'm right there because I don't want anyone to think, God forbid, I'm a mother and I have to go home. I don't want my work to suffer. I don't want that perception. They gave me two months off and I worked from home for one of them. And there's no question that when I came back I had to do some real damage control."

The much-discussed Mommy Track is another price women pay for working on men's terms. When I became pregnant, a woman I know—an expert in work and family issues—urged me to take a lesser position and cut down on my stress. "This is not the time to try for more," she announced. Luckily, I was too hardheaded and intent on doing a good job to heed her advice. I took on a big assignment, and the joy I took out of its success kept me buoyant through the very hard first year of my son's life. Had I not had work that was interesting and challenging, I would have been too focused on how tired I was and how hard I found the adjustment to motherhood. Instead, I had a bigger canvas in my life, I felt good about myself as a professional, and my son benefited as well. Psychologist and author Rosalind Barnett's study of women, men, and work backs up the way I felt. In her book, *He Works/She Works*, based on the study, she points out that Mommy Track jobs tend to be characterized by more routine work and less authority—two things that researcher Robert Karasek has proven cause increased stress.

The simple fact is that men who start families during this period have wives or significant others who, even if they work, are usually the ones who do the extra month of work a year[10] that career women put in managing home and office. To be equal to men at work, then, women often have to deny their home lives and responsibilities. Not to do so would put them at a disadvantage. And to do so puts them in a bind.

Breakdown

What all these pressures did for me was force the personal me and the professional me into opposing corners. Each morning the bell would ring and out would come these two identities, sparring with each other, fighting for the minutes on the clock and for my attention. The relationship between the two felt like the antagonistic bickering of two married people who love each other but can't live with each other but don't want to get divorced. The contract I'd made with my professional life wasn't holding up so well as I got older. When I'd made it, I hadn't anticipated that success would fragment my life and force me to make decisions that I felt diminished one side of me or another.

The limits of being a success on male terms sooner or later begin to wear us down, like waves pounding on the rocks. But this breakdown brings great gifts. It takes something this painful for us to depart from the great (and unrealistic) expectations we had of ourselves. Only when we become really miserable are we willing to abandon the antagonistic roles we are trying to perfect. Only then can we begin reclaiming who we are and what is important to us. We grow. The system doesn't. Something has to give.

CHAPTER 4

When Work Stops Working

BECAUSE I COULDN'T IMAGINE LIFE WITH-
out my work, I was willing to be pretty miserable in order to hold
on to the tokens of traditional accomplishment that I'd spent
almost two decades accumulating. It was going to have to get
really bad before I quit and left behind my professional identity,
my work friends, and my creative outlet. Like one of Cinderella's
wicked stepsisters I was willing to waltz around with tortured feet
before I would even entertain leaving the ball. Besides, if I left,
who on earth would I be? And if I "downshifted," would I become less of what I once was?

I'd love to say that when I started to see that my career had
limits, I picked myself up, dusted myself off, and changed my life.
It wasn't so simple. In fact, I spent several years desperately trying
different things to make it work. But because the value my life
was so deeply tied in to how well I was doing in my career, I
couldn't leave it or change it. I was held hostage by success.

That long last dance with my career wasn't so different from a relationship I'd had in my late twenties with a guy I'll call Richard. An extremely nice man, Richard was, on paper, everything I was supposed to marry—educated, moral, kind, and very, very wealthy. Both of us found in the other the person our parents and society had prepared us to wed. The problem was, we really didn't love each other. Rather than admit this fact and save everyone a good deal of time and heartache, we moved in together. I was determined to ignore what my gut was saying because my gut just had to be wrong. There was too much external proof that this guy was perfect for me. *What's wrong with you?* I remember thinking. *He's got everything.* If I wasn't in love with *this* guy, then something most definitely had to be wrong with me. I hung in there for a long time, trying to get the scales to balance. On one side was the nice man, great real estate (he had three homes), and permanent financial security. On the other side, my hazy doubts and nebulous feelings that didn't exactly add up to a feeling of love for him. Richard and I wasted five years trying to strong-arm our hearts into cooperation.

Looking back, I can now clearly see the bind I was in. I did not possess the self-confidence to respect my reservations and turn away someone who had nothing visibly wrong with him (someone who was society's definition of "a good catch"), nor did I have an ounce of faith that I'd be okay if I did leave the relationship. Instead, I dived into the either/or pit—I either stuffed my feelings and chose a "successful" union or I fell deeply, blackly, into spinsterhood and failure. And while I was making up my mind, I held my life hostage, waiting and hoping reality would change.

When that relationship finally drew its last breath, I threw myself all the harder into my career. I was now doubly determined to be successful so that I could have all the things I'd lost forever in my failed attempt to marry security. This was during the time when it seemed that all the books that were being published were about women who depended too much on men for their identities. I smugly congratulated myself on having dodged that particular bullet. Of course I didn't see that my relationship with my career was quickly starting to bear the same stamp as those male/female relationships. Instead of depending on a guy, I depended on something else external—my title, salary, company—to give me the sense of who I was and what I was worth (not to mention social and financial security).

During this period my external life got better and better. I really felt proud of myself; I'd accomplished a great deal. But the shortfalls in the rest of my life were becoming very apparent. After Richard and I mutually dumped each other I had very little life outside work. Most of my friends were now busy trying to raise kids and keep working. The three remaining unmarried girlfriends and I would go to the movies occasionally and we'd attend parties together. I dated a succession of men who were about as indifferent to me as I was to them. I began to settle in to the reality that my work was going to be the most sustaining relationship in my life. And when I looked at it in that light, it didn't look so swell.

Past my mid-thirties I didn't see many rungs above me on the ladder. The one I was on had brought me to a level where more and more was being asked of my time and my soul. If I wanted kids, I was going to have to carve out some time to throw the dating thing into high gear. Time passed more quickly, it

seemed; its shadow consumed my opportunities. I knew I had
come to the place where every move I made or didn't make
created a permanent consequence. My career now carried as
many problems as solutions, and a cold paralysis inched up my legs
and moved to a place where my joy had recently been. Outwardly, I was living the good life but it had stopped feeling good
anymore.

I sat in that point of breakdown for several years before I had
the courage and faith to do something about it. As the awareness
of my discontent grew, my doubts increased but so did my denial
and my determination. I was going to make things work out. No
matter what.

I rigidly dismissed alternatives to the traditional picture of
success. Anyone who departed from the path—well, it was fine
for them, but not for me. Maybe I felt I had sacrificed too much
personally in my quest for achievement. Maybe I still wanted
everything. Most likely, however, it was just too threatening to
start questioning the thing that formed the core of who I was.
After close to two decades of daily emotional, physical, and spiritual investment, what if I discovered I really was in the wrong
profession? Or worse, that I had fallen out of love with the right
one and had nowhere else I wanted to go? I feared that if I
weren't what I did for a living, I'd be no one at all. Fear made me
resist examination.

As I grew increasingly irritable with my day-to-day life, I felt
stuck, suspended between two options: continue as I was or make
some radical changes. Neither sounded good to me. I wanted to
do what I was doing but have more fun. Be less pressured. Since I
worked in a profession in which people frequently changed com-

panies, I tried that a few times. But as I moved around, I began to see my problems went deeper than which letterhead sat on the top of my stationery. The real problem was that I couldn't imagine how to have a life and have success with its rewards of money (a nice home), power (freedom), and status (high social regard). I wasn't willing to risk everything I'd worked for on the off chance my inner life, my personal life, whatever you want to call it, might be more fulfilling. As in my relationship with Richard, I found myself hostage once again to my sense of what I thought was expected of me.

Anna Quindlen remembers a woman who responded to a speech she gave about leaving *The New York Times:* " 'This is all very well and good for you to leave your job,' the woman said, 'but what about people who are supporting their families?' " Quindlen was glad that the question was asked, because it's a genuine issue. "If you can't do it, if you have to take care of the mortgage payment, then that takes care of business," responded Quindlen. But afterward, when the woman came up to talk, it turned out that she was the general counsel of one of the largest companies in the country. "That woman's problem wasn't the mortgage. She can't make a change because there is a part of her brain that is held hostage to what the world construes as success," Quindlen observed. "What she's got to do is take the gun barrel away from that part of her brain and say, 'Wait a minute. When I'm on my deathbed, I'm not going to say to myself, "Gee, everyone out there really thought that I was a success." I'm going to have to say to myself, "Did I do what I wanted to do with my life?" ' And if the answer is no, God help you. That's got to be one of the saddest moments of your life. That's the thing I feel good about. That I can say to myself, 'For good or ill, in good times and bad times, I've really cut my own path.'"

That general counsel could have been almost any woman with whom I've lunched in the past five years, or any woman interviewed for this book. It's as if the whole group of us were standing on the bank of a river looking at different lives on the far shore. But none of us wants to jump in the water. Instead we stand on the edges looking wistfully at the other side and we tell each other all the scary things about the water. "It's cold, it's wet, the current is swift, there are things that bite in there." We have a thousand things that we let stand between us and what we say we want. We resist the risk. We resist the change. We resist leaving the security of the identity we know. How human.

Betrayal

I stayed glued to the seat of my office chair during this break-down, held by the loyalty I had for my original picture of a successful life—the one with the great job and the great family life. As I sat there, not only was my life not great, but things around me seemed to be getting worse too. My profession was changing rapidly and objectively—and not for the good. The positions that had once looked like destinations of security and recognition were starting to resemble first-class deck chairs on the *Titanic*. Friends who were extremely talented got fired. Icons of publishing were being hustled to the door, treated without dignity and respect. "If it could happen to them . . ." we all whispered among ourselves. Instead of finding a haven of respect and security at the end of the long climb up the ladder, we now saw a place from which any one of us could be dropped at any time. A sense of fearfulness started to seep into what we did. We saw how expendable everyone had become.

"I hate to say this, but I feel betrayed, somehow," says Nancy, who is a forty-five-year-old executive for a division of a major manufacturer. "But why? What do I think betrayed me? Who? And what right do I, who have money in the bank, a pension, and a nice home, what right do I have to complain?" When I first met her, Nancy had just found out that her division, a new venture for the company, was about to disappear. And what stung her the most was that her management had made the decision without including her. While Nancy was assured that she'd have a job, the new position offered was several levels lower than her current one. "They said I have to get back into the *core* business," says she sarcastically. "So people can get to know me again. When I was in the new venture, they kept telling me that what I was doing was equal to what others were doing in the main business, but that didn't turn out to be the case. I'm going back where I was five years ago." Nancy is particularly upset by the way her staff is being treated—rather shabbily. Most bewildering, however, is that her division was not only making money but exceeding the business plan.

Alison, a contemporary of Nancy's, echoes her feelings. "Bait and switch. I feel like what happened to me was bait and switch," she says angrily. "They said, 'Go to business school! Get an MBA! Get on the track and go for that brass ring!' So I got on the track and when I got close to the ring they said, 'Sorry, we're going to change the rules now, you need to work harder, take on more, wait longer for the rewards. We're going to speed this baby up a bit. You're going to have to move down, do more, and then, maybe the ring.' I feel like I fought on the battle lines for the opportunity and privilege of exploiting myself. I got close to the top and realized that no one was going to appreciate me for all my hard work, certainly not love me. And given the times, all that's going to happen is that with each success they're going to want more. This sure as hell isn't what I imagined."

Like Alison, Nancy was stuck too. She couldn't imagine life without her career, but she couldn't stomach life with it. "What can I do? I can quit. But it's no better anywhere else. There is nowhere else in my business where it's better than here. Besides, I don't want to quit. What would I do with my life? This *is* my life. I can go find a new job, but there are no guarantees there, or I can take this new position, grin and bear it, and show them what a good sport I can be. None of these look particularly good to me. It's hard to know what to do because I'm so totally burned out. I'm not thinking so clearly."

Nancy's and Alison's stories are like many others I heard in which women get to a certain point in their careers only to find that the rules have changed. Instead of the security we saw our fathers having, we started to be afraid of being fired for the first time in our careers. Not because we weren't good at our jobs but because some company bought us, or we were merged, or made redundant for cost-cutting reasons. Just as we got to a point where we could enjoy the fruits of all our hard work, corporation became less generous, the paternalism that once offered a feeling of being taken care of was done in by squeezed profit margins.

This change left Nancy bereft. "I gave this job my body and my soul and now I can't get my soul back." She sighs. "I'm hung up on this recognition thing. I can't believe I have worked this long and this hard and I still expect someone to say, 'Hey, Nancy, great job. We really appreciate your contribution and for all you've done for the company we're going to include you more and give you a title that reflects our confidence in you and respect.' Instead I get 'Hey, Nancy. If you want to keep your job, you have to take this lesser one.' I just feel the whole game has changed and I have no options but to go with it."

Many women's situations aren't as dramatic as Nancy's; but like her, we didn't anticipate that job security was going to become an issue for the first time in the middle of our careers. We began working to keep the work, not for the love of it. This change in the corporate climate coincided with most women's achievement leaving them feeling squeezed between increased responsibility and vanishing rewards. "Work started to lose its meaning just as we got our power," Jane observed in a conversation we had almost a year after she left her first career. "Everyone was running around scared; no one was enjoying work. For a long time we believed that we could be satisfied with work forever. But then it started to dawn on us that we weren't going to get the power or respect we hoped for. Can't say I miss all that."

By this time many of us begin asking, "Is this all there is? Is this what *I* want for *my* life?" When the guarantees of security and recognition were threatened or made extinct by the change in the business climate, our "personal" dreams—postponed or submerged in the name of building a recognizably good life—started to bob to the surface. The gold standard of success had tarnished. We started to look at our lives in a different light. (The younger women coming up behind us have a different but equally daunting task: they forge forward with the full knowledge that the corporate world only cares about the corporate world. With eyes opened by the realities of layoffs and downsizing, the lack of meaningful work alternatives for these women means that they are often beginning their careers knowing the limits.)

Far from being an immediately liberating experience, this causes a profound crisis for women. At this point we're very invested, psychologically and financially, with work. We see we've tied our sails to a rock. We can't imagine not working but the path we're on doesn't lead to where we hoped it would go. Because we have lived with the concept of More Is Better for so long, wanting a life with less of something—even if that something is stress—takes on the stain of failure. We start to see the paradox of achievement: we don't necessarily want more of what we have, yet we don't have a society that supports that kind of thinking.

It's not accidental that we get to this point when we've achieved some measure of success. Part of this is due to the fact that the pace of our careers slows dramatically and we have a moment (maybe for the first time in years) to pause and look around. We find that we have mistaken movement for satisfaction. "To be 'stuck' is a very different work experience from being on the move, from being 'up and coming,' " says Rosabeth Moss Kanter. "Too little opportunity, for example, may result in rapid decay of whatever interest or excitement is contained in a particular position, just as the uplifting effect of a raise may decline if no further raises appear to be forthcoming."[1] Things we were willing to overlook earlier in our career for the sake of advancement or the chance to do interesting work start to lose their camouflage and become very hard to ignore.

Another reason our perspective changes with accomplishment is that we women need to feel we have proven ourselves in order to feel secure enough to separate out what we do for a living from who we are as people. As author Terri Apter said, "Women's conditions had to improve before they complained. Women had to change their perceptions of their abilities and their expectations of their careers, and their sense of what is fair. They had to summon the strength to fight custom and prejudice of which their silence hitherto had been a product."[2] This perspective doesn't happen until we have either matured enough or achieved enough to suspect how much of ourselves we have traded for our success.

Because the process is cumulative and so subtle, it's hard to see how the cultural messages that have been continually broadcast to us have directed our lives. The submerging of private, personal values in favor of the dominant, approved, or expedient ones happens slowly, incident by incident. Women begin to see the pattern they have created only after many choices have been made. It takes experience and self-confidence to stand back and critically assess a system that we have relied on to develop our confidence in the first place. But as the evolution of women's roles in the workplace continues, it becomes clearer and clearer that at some point, our agendas depart in critical places from the self-sacrificing hero's value system.

Up until the point where I had unarguably succeeded in my

profession, there had been no room on my agenda for any item that contained a subversive alternative to success. I needed the approval and respect of my peers and bosses for my own sense of self-worth and I equated that recognition with success. But when I reached a place where I started to get some perspective, where I started to see what all my compromises really brought and that there were many more in store, the internal consequences of the trades I had made to have success (as my father would define success) became very clear. Maybe I got high enough to be able to see a panoramic snapshot of my life. Maybe it was the increasingly hectic nature of my life as my responsibilities proliferated exponentially. And maybe I started sensing my mortality as Jane did.

Critiquing the Agenda

For many women, at this point in our lives we clearly see that the agenda we had in our twenties—the one that reflected who we *thought* we should be—isn't holding up so well over time. Some of us have the great personal life and the so-so career. Others have the tremendous career and a compromised personal life. Still others have a little of both some of the time and a little of neither some of the time. Regardless, none of us has all of it all of the time. We see that balance is impossible and that we're going to have to make some hard choices. Marissa Clark, a thirty-nine-year-old Minneapolis commercial realtor, found she actually didn't even want what society's picture of success was. "I realized I had spent my life trying to get the world to affirm me because I felt so unaffirmed. I think that not having kids made me more determined; I suppose it was then more important for me to be more successful, because I was certainly aware that as a woman without children I was not meeting the criteria that I was brought up with to be known as a successful woman. Because if I don't have children, then I'm not successful. Period. Full stop.

"It's not even a conscious thing. It's an unconscious thing. I got the message that women without children were not full women. They were women who had not completed tasks assigned or to have made it in the culture's definition of what being a good American woman was. I went through the period of wanting children, struggling with the notion of having children and having a career and believing that I could do both. Then, I realized that there were problems with my health and that put a hold on my having children. And to be very honest, it was a relief." Marissa had been in a prolonged struggle with herself. She really didn't want children. Yet, she believed she would be a failure as a woman if she didn't have them. So she fought to override her own sense of what she knew was right for her. Marissa also knew she wanted to be successful at work, yet the extra blood she tried to squeeze from it in order to make up for the imagined insufficiencies in the rest of her life had drained her love of her job. What Marissa really wanted to do was switch careers and become a social worker. But she was afraid that if she went to a less prestigious career, then she'd be seen as a failure in all parts of her life. She needed her high-powered job, she thought, to have any social station at all. To have any worthwhile identity. But as she stayed in real estate knowing she wanted to do something else, she became more and more depressed. She began to lose her way of judging if her life was okay anymore. Like other women who reach this breakdown point, she had to live for a while with the uncomfortable awareness that there were two different value systems clamoring to guide her one life. The result was a period when she had a real sense of failure and deflation.

For Marissa all the cards were now on the table. She wanted a new life, she knew she would have to trade in the old. Women who hit this point have the perspective and experience to see there's a price paid any way we go—whether we choose our work over our personal lives or our personal lives over our careers. At this point the competition between the two worlds—the career and the personal—becomes concrete. Even the work itself starts to suffer as the energy that would have gone into the work is instead diverted to managing the tension that this adversarial relationship produces. Yet women can and do live in this place for years, as I did. We see that the consequence of holding to our original agenda is decreased happiness, but we are unable to draw up a new one yet. It's painful to see clearly and feel powerless to act.

Starting to Live from the Inside Out

"Not until my thirties did I begin to suspect that there might be an internal power I was neglecting," recollects Gloria Steinem. "Though the way I'd grown up had encouraged me to locate power almost anywhere but within myself, I began to be increasingly aware of its pinpoint of beginning within—my gender and my neighborhood notwithstanding."[3] It's a radical and scary notion—that our personal power might be equal to our professional

100

power and that we might have an inner agenda that differs from society's expectations. It's unnerving because we have depended for most of our lives on external things to shape and define us. We've given enormous power to the institutions (and their agents) around us. But once it starts to dawn on us that we've gotten to where we are on our own talents and not by luck or through the good graces and generosity of our superiors, we experience a change in perspective that alters everything. For years we've had to keep our focus on what our superiors thought of us. We had to because management is a power game, it grants the promotions, withholds time off, gives special exemptions, and determines the pace and shape of our progress. It's not surprising, then, that we tend to locate the source of our good fortune outside ourselves. Yet, at this point, we have achieved enough that we begin to understand that our talents are our own and our strengths are independent of our teachers, mentors, and managers. We start to see we, too, are powerful.

The largest obstacle to this perspective had been this reliance on outside forces and institutions to affirm and define us. As long as that dependence existed, we didn't take credit for our hard work. Thus, when our lives didn't turn out as expected, we blamed ourselves, not the institutions and the value systems that kept them propped up. Janet Andre is a consultant for women and work; in her years of experience she found that for most women who had not gotten what they wanted professionally, "they think *It's because of me, it's something I've done personally. I wasn't aggressive enough or I didn't do well enough on a project.* They blame themselves." Career counselor Shoya Zichy agrees: "Women think that their situations are their fault. They put the responsibility on themselves: 'Why am I not happy here?' they question. 'I've been given all the opportunities, why?' "

Yet this failure to make it all work out is a tremendous turning point. It is the exact moment at which women can separate who we are from what we do. We can reclaim our personal abilities and talents. Most women suspect that our lives are limited by circumstances—either personal or professional. In fact, it is usually women's inordinate abilities that have allowed this out-of-balance situation to exist as long as it has. If we weren't so capable, our lives would have fallen apart long ago. It is this shift in personal perspective that marks a profound turning point and reclamation for women.

Career strategist and author of *Skills for Success,* Adele Scheele tells the story of a midwestern women's college whose president had asked her for advice. The reports they had been collecting on their graduated nurses showed that they were failing in the workplace—either leaving their jobs, or being fired. Either way there was a tremendous turnover and consternation. What should they do? Why were they failing? What part did the college play? When Scheele looked closely at the data, she realized the college was doing everything right. The nurses who had graduated were different nurses trained elsewhere. They just didn't follow orders given to them by rote; they had trained to be critical thinkers. Scheele sees a real parallel between these nurses and the accomplished career women. The very skills that brought them success enabled them to become critical thinkers. Once they apply that ability to themselves, they feel they don't fit in or don't want to fit in to their work environments anymore. The failure they feel, however, is actually the starting point of tremendous change. Only when we experience a breakdown in expectations and rewards can the woman underneath the persona who has been clothed in layers of organizational conformity start to question the fashion.

Freedom

It's at this point that we receive the biggest gift of the collapse of our relationship with work. Along with a new feeling of self-confidence we also see that we aren't the problem. We're just departing from an old script. "It was like when I realized that the problems in my marriage were my husband's and not mine," said a recently divorced attorney. "All of a sudden it wasn't the ten pounds I never took off after our child was born or that he was threatened because I had a career of my own. Maybe seeing that helped me understand that there was something wrong with the firm I worked for as well. When a client dinner is more important than taking my kid to camp for the first time, there's something wrong with that, not with me."

When our futures and happiness come down to either/or choices—either we stay in a situation that is dragging us down and making us miserable or we risk real change—it suddenly seems possible to rebuild a life based on the little bits of deferred dreams and pieces of personal expression that we consigned to a wish list long ago. "When they see they aren't the problem—that the problem lies with the system—when they find that out, then that releases so much of them," states Shoya Zichy, who has seen this happen to women repeatedly. "All the skills it took them to get there now become huge assets."

The change in perception that occurs colors everything. The doggedness that many women found criticized as unflatteringly aggressive or "tough" now becomes a platform for beginning a new independent business. The kind of problem-solving thinking that tried to fix things within the conventional system that did not want to be fixed now becomes a powerful tool for personal change. In other words, all the things women took apart in themselves in trying to see why work wasn't working for them are restored to them whole. These abilities were just not the problem.

With this recognition, however, the fears rush in. Because we know that we're going to have to reject a value system we've lived with all our lives, one that dominates our culture. It's understandable that we wonder if we've gone nuts. We face all the very real demons of economic insecurity, loss of status, loss of identity. We have, after all, a world around us that exerts tremendous pressure on us to stay where we are and keep doing what we're doing. Once the question of change rises up, a swell of resistance rises to meet it. If we aren't careful, our new inner direction can be drowned in the forceful sea of the status quo.

CHAPTER 5

Resistance at
the Turning Point

IT TOOK ME A WHILE TO SEPARATE MY love for my work from my fear of not having any. Until I did that, I resisted making any changes. Resistance was a marvelous teacher. It laid out the obstacles between where I was (pretty unhappy with my life) and where I was afraid to go (home? out on my own? to a new company? a new career?). Before I could make real and lasting changes in my life, I had to know what was keeping me attached to the one I was living now.

If we are really serious about getting to a point where work works for us, we have to plunge into the water and see what the reality of our resistance is; otherwise we will continue to be held hostage on the shore of our fears. In her book *Thinking Out Loud* Anna Quindlen cites something Dorothy Thompson said in 1939: "One cannot exist today as a person—one cannot exist in full consciousness—without having to have a showdown with one's self, without having to define what it is that one lives by, without being clear in one's own mind what it is that one lives by, without being clear in one's own mind what matters and what does not matter."[1]

To do what Thompson advocates involves taking stock of where we are, what we like about it and what we don't. It means that we have to be ready to switch from the accepted system of recognizable success to something more individually rewarding. It means living by our own values and sometimes that requires some substantial sacrifices. To make this enormous shift takes courage and usually lots of misery. But until we make the commitment, most of us find we are stuck in a state of profound inertia, paralyzed by the fact that we're going to have to give something up. We also want to know we are doing the right thing. This kind of emotional traffic jam can go on for a long time, but it is an enormous opportunity for us to take stock of our lives and draw up a new agenda for ourselves. Meanwhile, all the mixed messages about who we think we are supposed to be clamor in our ears. It's a confusing time, a scary time. But it's an important stage in the process of finding work that works. Only by facing the real and imagined obstacles in our lives are we going to get to the other side. "The best way out is always through," said Ralph Waldo Emerson. Easy for him to say.

Decisions and Turning Points

Mary Perkins sits in the eye of the storm of an enormous corporate merger examining two organization charts. Each one resembles the other. Mary knows there are people behind those boxes and that in a few days, she will be asked to choose among them.

At the same time, she realizes that someone a few floors above her is also looking at a piece of paper with her box on it too. "Our company just merged with another huge company and right now there is all this spaghetti on the walls and nobody knows what's going to stick and who's going to have jobs," she says. Her office has bare walls and "new" furniture inherited from a recently downsized executive. "I'm in the middle of a crisis and I've got to make some big decisions about whether I'm going to ride this out, see what happens and take whatever is offered, or bail out entirely. I hate this; I hate this; I hate this."

Mary knows that if she decides to stay she will be working even harder under the newly merged megacorporation. If she opts out, she has no idea what will happen, or who she will be. She has arrived at what she calls her "something's-gotta-give period," which means either her career or her personal life is going to get smaller for the good of the other. Yet, as Mary struggles to make a clear decision, she encounters resistance as she contemplates every option. Who she is and what she does are such deep parts of her identity and security that she can't imagine any kind of change—even one that might make her happier. As a consequence Mary is stuck, suspended in midcareer, midlife, midair.

She recognizes that what looks like a career choice is actually a deeper dilemma. "My problem isn't so much professional, because I can apply my brain to anything; I can do almost any job," she acknowledges. "My problem is what do I really want spiritually and emotionally? I can do whatever job they want me to do, but at what price? The question is not whether or not I am dedicated or whether I can succeed and go all the way with the brass ring, it's what do I really want my life to be? When you create choices, you have different options. It's quite different when you create a life for your family or you create a life for your work."

Mary has arrived at the turning point where she has to make some decisions that will have very real and long-term consequences. She wishes she had her values and priorities sorted out, because making a decision would be much easier. But she confesses that until her back was to the wall, she delayed making painful choices. Now, everything is whirling together—her sense of who she is, what she wants, what she needs, and what the world expects of her. Sitting in the center of this storm, she finds it hard to decide which direction to go in—back where she came from, or into an entirely new place. She recalls how she felt when her father was extremely ill. He said to her then, "Your job is your job and your life is your life. Don't mix the two up." She now tells that to people who work for her. She understands that jobs and bosses come and go. But when it comes to putting that wisdom to work in her own life, it's not so simple.

Mary is struggling to find the strength to live that way, but to do so she needs to find out what's really driving her. "I struggle with it every day," she admits. "It's not like it's a final decision and I say, 'Now I am driven by my values.' I struggle with it all the time, I struggle with 'Will I make the right decision? Do I really want to be some kind of a power broker? Do I want to move to a smaller home and spend more time with my family? Other of my friends are running companies now, have I missed the boat?' I deal with that all the time. But at my core I really know that my values are what's driving my life right now and not the other way around. I feel more in control because of it, but I still have a lot to sort out. I have a twin sister who is going through similar stuff. There is a pattern here. You begin to think about it and ask yourself, *What are we really doing here? Is it about the work? Is it about the money? What is it about?"*

The Spinning Value Compass

As Mary investigates the answers to these questions, she finds clarity elusive. The needle on her value compass keeps getting spun around by internal and external static. Internally, there is fear: fear of financial insecurity, of loss of status, of loss of purpose, of loss of identity. Externally, Mary knows that she can't just walk out of her job; she is the principal wage earner, the provider of benefits. Her lifestyle depends on her income and she has suspicions that being a full-time mother isn't for her. It's hard to get a good sense of direction when so much inside and outside of her resists change.

"It's that fear time where I have to struggle with that transition of *Okay. I can do it another way*. That's what I haven't come to grips with yet," she says. She's not quite ready to make the changes she suspects would bring her fulfillment, changes that might result in a different life. She has invested so much in the one she has, she is reluctant to let go. She suspects that one of the reasons she is waiting to see what happens in her company is so she won't have to make a decision that means stepping off the traditional path to success. In a sense, if events take care of the decision for her, then all she has to do is deal with the change. "Unfortunately, for most of my life I have waited for external triggers. In most cases I think women have to be pushed to the wall," she says. "We don't want to make that choice. We want it made for us. And when it is, you go through the miserable transition period and then you come out the other side happier and healthier. But we don't want to make this choice."

Because success itself has become our identity, to diminish any part of our profession is equal to diminishing ourselves. We depend on our work to define us. This understanding completely colors the nature of Mary's crisis. For her decision isn't just whether she will stay or go. It's about what she would be letting go of and about defining what is really important in her life. It's about developing courage to go along with her values that will chart her course toward the spiritual wholeness and life of balance and fulfillment she says she desires so strongly.

"There is no paradigm or role model to look to either," she concludes. "There are role-model people, but you can't interpret what to do from their lives because there always is a different combination of variables. You have to interpret it for yourself. There are no easy answers. And it's a pretty isolated exercise. It's an evolution which is exciting, but it's not easy."

It's not surprising that Mary's feelings run back and forth between peril and promise. It feels dangerous to question the conventional value system whose measure of success is money, status, and power. Besides, we like the things and privileges that money and status yield. Yet, when we reach the moment of decision, we are presented with the chance to reclaim power over the way we value our own lives.

When we contemplate making changes that could affect how much we make, what we do every day, how people will value us, and how we perceive ourselves, we end up questioning how important those things are to us. We are challenging the values we live by. What do we really believe? Does our life reflect those beliefs? If not, what is standing in the way? What looks deceptively like a simple change in the structure of our daily activities really involves making a deep internal shift in the value and priority we assign to almost everything in our lives.

One of the disorienting aspects of this ambivalent moment is that it forces us to look at "facts" in our lives we never before questioned. Diving below the surface, we discover we have given great value to things that aren't anchored to anything more than convention or what the Joneses have. We have endowed our participation in the five-day, "forty-hour" workweek—an outdated structure of history, not necessity—with all sorts of shades of moral virtue. We grew up believing that being a hard worker meant being a good person. Every woman surveyed agreed that working hard was important, yet few had ever really questioned the structure of that work or, if they had, found viable alternatives. After discussing this in one focus group, one woman said, "Gee. Who died and made the sixty-hour week the one true way?" Almost no one interviewed said she had ever made a financial plan based on desires rather than perceived needs. And when she had, it was because, as one New Jersey woman said, "I just couldn't go on the way I was going. If I didn't simplify my life, I wasn't going to have one at all."

In spite of the fact that more than half the women in my study felt that "work didn't work for them anymore," more than two thirds of them had done absolutely nothing about it. Of these women one third said they didn't know what else they would like to do. Another third felt they had invested so much of their lives in their careers, they couldn't see starting over. The final third said they really couldn't afford to change. In other words, although financial concerns are real, women felt that questions of identity and desire were equally important factors in keeping them in work they said didn't work for them.

Resistances

In focus groups, sooner or later, women would get around to talking about the vision of how they wanted their lives to be. Each one had that value compass inside that pointed her in a certain direction. Each direction was different for each woman, but there were some overall similarities. All of the women wanted to work, but they wanted the work to be more meaningful. They wanted to work in environments with less hierarchy, that were less male dominated, more flexible and caring. They all wanted more time for family and friends, and less stress. Most felt they were making too little contribution to their communities. Many dismissed these visions, though, as impractical or impossible—they submerged the possibility of living that way so deeply under obligation and duty that scarcely an air bubble rose to the conscious surface anymore. These women looked to the value of mortgages or rents, car payments and school tuitions, as dictating the course of their days. They diminished the value of their desires and those things that they thought would fulfill them by not acting on them. Besides, if they did try and live their dreams, many of the women admitted they could hear in their heads the voices of one or both parents saying, "Just *who* do you think *you* are? Of course work is hard. That's why they call it work." That alone was enough to shame most women into a dead stop. Even putting ancestral messages aside, woman after woman told stories of how society itself seemed to conspire against change.

You Are What You Do: What Society Sees

Marie Wilson, president of the Ms. Foundation, tells the story of how, as a young mother of five, she would go to cocktail parties with her husband. "I was married to a musician and we had all these children and I wasn't in the work force. In my husband's world, if you weren't a musician you were a nobody. I would go to all these functions and the minute they found out I wasn't a musician, I didn't exist. I was invisible. One night I went to a function and a woman said to me, 'What do you do?' and I replied that I had five children. She said, 'Well, maybe you can help me with potty training.' She was trying to find *something* about me that was useful."

Women know this question of identity is probably their central concern—all they have to do is look at themselves through another's eyes and see mirrored the conflicting messages women get about what makes them valued. Under the hero's terms, what we do more or less determines who we are and what we are worth in the hierarchy of things. Since the model's first job is to perpetuate itself, work is most holy. It follows that the more important our work—i.e. the more money, success, and power that falls from that work—the more important we are.

In a sense, that identity message propelled women into the

workforce as strongly as did the desire for economic freedom. The fight for professional equality was also a fight for women to be held as *valuable* as men were. Yet, the system that came up with the you-are-worth-what-you-do formula is precisely the same one that has given a lesser value to "women's work" and, by extension, to women. No wonder women resist any change that would involve stepping out of the traditional sphere of success. They that feel that way become devalued instantly. To resist that is to be deeply sane.

Gender-Based Devaluation or "Just Like a Woman"

"There's still a tendency when people question the greater assumptions of the society or the value of the corporate structure to find some way to denigrate that choice." Anna Quindlen speaks from experience. When she decided to trade in her prestigious and powerful position to become a full-time novelist, she ran into a wall of commentary that tried to explain away her choice. "Some of the people who wanted to know why I left asked my friends, 'Did Anna find out she was being passed over for the top editor's job?' It couldn't be that I said, *'The New York Times* is a great institution, but some things about it don't meet my needs anymore.' It had to be 'She couldn't cut the mustard' or 'At base she's really a girl.' In order to make sense of it they had to estrogenize it. It couldn't be that there was a greater source of satisfaction based on your own assessment of what you want. Instead it was 'She wanted to spend more time on the playground,' which completely ignores the fact that I've spent so much of my time on the playground over the last twelve years that I can seesaw and think about welfare reform at the same time without breaking a sweat."

Any woman considering anything other than a terminal climb up the career ladder invariably encounters versions of Quindlen's experience. Cindy Mason recalls that a well-meaning friend once told her husband, "Never assume two salaries. One day she will want to quit and stay home." Cindy admits she stayed in law school and then worked as a lawyer for longer than she wished in part because she wanted to prove she could "cut it." She wanted to prove that men like the one who had advised her husband were wrong about women like Cindy. Needless to say, when she finally did take a break, on top of her concerns about money, identity, and career, she had to shovel through the shame she felt about proving that man right.

When Alicia Daymans, a forty-two-year-old art director, told her father about her plan to take a position of less responsibility, "he said to me—actually, mostly men have said to me—'Tell them you left because of your daughter. Who can argue with that?'" My father urged me to start looking for another job three months after I'd started writing this book but before I had a contract. It was his way of showing his love for me, making sure I didn't expire sitting on the shelf. His idea of work just doesn't have any examples of voluntary interruptions in it. For anyone who questions the status quo, the laws of physics apply: for every action there is an equal and opposite reaction. The forces of resistance we overcame to get us into our careers now act to keep us from questioning them.

Any change that doesn't bring more—more money, more power, more status—is suspect. Even the very term *downshifting* implies a diminution, a lessening. We don't call it "upgrading" or "enlarging," which are the downshifter's quality-of-life goals. Rejecting what society values as the moral, right path of success is a dangerous act. It's rebellious, treasonous; it causes people to defend or define their way of valuing life. If you reject it, you reject them. The immediate defense is to devalue your intentions and actions.

In one group of women interviewed (all of whom had either left or changed their place of work in the financial community), each had a story to tell about how her management tried to make it look as if she had left because of "female reasons." "I heard that I was leaving because I was getting married," fumed one woman, Dorothy, who was really leaving because it became very clear she was never going to be promoted. She left to start her own invest-ment banking firm. Jean, who at fifty had been one of the most senior women in her firm, recalled that "my leaving was posi-tioned as a desire to stay home and be a wife and mother. Right. After twenty-three years I had a sudden change of life. Like it had nothing to do with the fact that I was sick of being surrounded by men whose ethics were suspect—and that's kind—and everyone was looking the other way."

In discussion, woman after woman detailed how she felt her decisions were devalued. It was done sub rosa, to be sure, but the insinuation was there—that being female, they just weren't made of the right stuff to "take it" (like a man). Usually, the inference was that they were emotional (i.e., "female") or that the maternal instinct had ultimately triumphed over the ability to be a good businessperson. Anger at unequal opportunity is seen as emo-tional; as is any expression of disgust at insensitive management.

116

Leaving a position to get away from an unethical or questionable business practice or a sexualized work environment becomes the "lack of a sense of humor" or an inability to "cut it." Wanting fewer hours for personal reasons or more flexibility for children becomes synonymous with a lessened ability to perform. As long as the male-provider model is seen as "normal" it will remain the standard, and any departure from it makes us "less" than those who accept it without outward disagreement.

Because we tend to question the system only when something rivals it in importance, we face the prospect of being devalued for some of the very qualities we know are important to us. It's disorienting and causes great internal tension when standing up for what you think is a better way makes you a less "valuable" or successful person. The system takes no prisoners; although there are increasing exceptions (as men push to change the system, the system must relent a little), for the most part, those who don't make the proper show of pursuing success cede failure.

Structural Resistance

The very structure of work itself frustrates any attempt to build a more balanced life based on other values besides work. Inertia, tradition, and the need for control combine to create a system that resists flexibility. Marcia Brumit Kropf, Ph.D., is the vice president of research and advisory services for Catalyst, a nonprofit organization that works with business and the professions to effect change for women. In 1996 she finished a major study on work structures that resulted in the publication *Making Work Flexible: Policy to Practice.*[2] She says that the standard "workplace structures are designed for the employees of yesterday." Ask any woman who has tried to shorten or rearrange her work schedule to include what she laughingly refers to as "a personal or home life." If it is possible at all, the first consequence is likely to be that she is no longer taken seriously. (One man interviewed in a focus group said that he absolutely would have to be physically ill to ask for reduced hours without facing a severe social and professional penalty.) Lucy Cohen, a thirty-seven-year-old marketing coordinator for a large pharmaceutical company, says that when she went to a four-day schedule, she "stopped registering on people's radar screens. It was like I had dropped out of orbit entirely. It was so clear I was no longer a 'player' because I said something else was more important than staying at work seventy hours a week. I broke the rules and got thrown out of the club." Even so, Lucy was considered "lucky" even to have the opportunity to go part time with its attendant privileges of loss of status and loss of opportunity, not to mention loss of crucial benefits.

The value placed on the number of hours we work usually forces anyone who wishes to do it a little differently into the position of looking like he or she isn't taking the work seriously. "You don't want to be seen as making a choice that something is more important than the work," says Kropf. "That's what drives a lot of people to stay in the workplace. I think there has to be a real focus on exposing and educating people on their values." Kropf says that there are many companies now that intellectually realize their companies need to change. "You read the policies and statements of commitment and you think, *Aha, terrific,*" says Kropf. "But few people will take advantage of those policies or programs because they feel the impact will be on how committed they're seen, how loyal they're seen, how intensely connected they are to their profession." Kropf believes that a shift of values has to precede any structural change, because otherwise we come right up against the old values that require long hours and "face time" for any recognition, reward, or advancement.

Even the corporate reporting structure cements certain values in place. "The traditional model is that there is somebody who is in charge of somebody else and it goes all the way up the ladder," observes Kropf. "It's command and control: 'I only trust you a little bit so I need to make sure you are here and I need to tell you what to do and I need to find out that you've done it well.' " That model usually leaves up to the supervisor the criteria for whether or not the employee is doing well and, by extension, whether or not the employee can do a plum assignment, receive a visible commission, or advance to the next level. Naturally, under that kind of system, people are reluctant to do anything that would jeopardize their relationship with their boss. Even though everyone has a boss, and most people agree this traditional system based on lack of trust is potentially demeaning and also leads to fragile communication paths, this traditional structure is still the most common. And it resists change: by the time people get through the hazing process to positions of relative or real power, they have become part of the system itself. Even if they don't like it, they value it—it has given them all they have today.

Anna Quindlen stresses how sensitive an area this is. If you are trying to either leave or change the system and you happen to be a mother, "what you are essentially saying to these people is 'You were a substandard parent.' Every time you say that you want to change work for more balance, the subliminal message is 'You

119

were not a good father.' Even if you don't mean it that way, I can guarantee you that they hear it that way on a certain level."

Although family is often the most pressing reason to alter the work structure, other reasons are equally resisted. A sixth-year law associate Kropf interviewed said she wanted to work ten months and teach two months a year to renew her brain, keep her enthusiasm up, alter the grind of the work. Because her partners hadn't done it that way, it wasn't an option for her. If she wanted to make partner, then she was going to have to toe the line.

Aside from the you-have-to-be-in-it-to-win-it attitude, there are real built-in penalties for alternatives. Benefits are available only with full-time employment, which for Americans means more than three days a week. Now that more than half of the women surveyed in several polls say they are the principal providers, the burden of maintaining benefits fall to them. A woman alone cannot afford to sacrifice a pension, a woman with a dependent family must have health insurance. With white-collar unemployment becoming an entrenched reality in America and Europe, women who try to alter the structure for more flexibility stand in the shadow of ready replacement.

Home offices, E-mail, telecommuting, and other "alternative" work arrangements hold out enticing possibilities for structural change, but they are being heavily resisted because they result in a loss of control, as Marie Wilson points out. "The thing I found in the 1970s when I first started to work on alternative working arrangements was that if you started to mess around with the structure of time in a corporation, it threatened everything. . . . A lot of us don't like the flat tax but a lot of us would like to jiggle a lot of what that would undo. Time is a component like that." She points out that the compensation and benefits structures are regulated governmentally in a way that frustrates reducing or prorating benefits based on alternative time-and-place arrangements. Changing those rules "would jiggle things up," she explains. "It would give workers unprecedented control of something—time—by which workers have been controlled." Ironically, even the unions are fighting a more flexible work world. In early 1997 a bill was introduced into Congress that would allow workers to work outside of the forty-hours, five-day-a-week structure created sixty years ago to ensure that people received proper pay. The unions, fearful that pay abuse would reenter the picture, fought hard to keep the present structure even though the composition of the work force was almost unrecognizably different from that of six decades ago. The value system that ties dollars to hours is still seen as more valuable than the one that allows for flexibility.

The psychological hold of the on-site, five-day-a-week, non–job sharing model is so strong that even women who have successfully started their own businesses sometimes admit they feel like "they are cheating" if they aren't working those long hours. Sue Weathers, a thirty-nine-year-old computer systems analyst, said, "I do a job, I work out at the gym. I make a luncheon meeting. I do the grocery shopping. I install a system, do a performance review, and get to my daughter's soccer game. My husband drags in from a two-day sales call. And I feel like he's been the one who's been working." We have inherited a way of valuing the structure of work that makes it very hard to value ourselves without it.

Reentry

It was subtle, but it was there. One year after I'd left my job, the telephone rang. An old employer was on the line calling to see if I was interested in taking a job that was several levels lower in responsibility, money, and status than my last position. "How's your son?" he asked. "Is he in school yet?" Unmistakable was the inference that my child was the reason for my staying home. "You know," he continued, "you haven't been working for a while. There aren't many people who would offer you something this good. You should carefully consider it." When I reminded him that I was actually home working, writing a book, he repeated that the longer I stayed at home, the harder it would be for me to get a job. I thanked him. I rung off. I shook my head a few times to knock out the mind pollution that had been planted there.

One of the most potent resistances that keep women from leaving a career path, even for a year or two, is the fear of not being able to get back on it. Reentry is a most effective structural resistance. Because work is structured linearly, careers are conducted by getting on a ladder and climbing up the levels of assistant, associate, manager, director, vice president. Miss a rung and a younger (usually male) person quickly scrambles into your place, closing the gap, extinguishing even the traces of your absence. "How do I explain my seven-year hiatus?" asks one mother of three, describing a job interview. "I looked across the table at some kid who a few years ago I might have interviewed as my assistant and thought, *What can I say? 'For the last seven years I've been mashing bananas and washing crayons off the wall. I'm bored with being up all night and I'm ready to go back to work'?* That's a winning interview. I know he is thinking that my thoughts are no longer 'current.' I'm not 'state of the art.' He says he is 'building a team' and I got the distinct feeling that my role would be den mother, not health-care professional. Besides, I have five times more experience than he does, and at a certain level I think he knew it."

In her speaking engagements around the country Anna Quindlen also found that reentry posed a huge concern for women. "It's the single biggest thing that comes up when I go out and give speeches," she says. "I give a speech about my mother dying and I say, 'I'm not going to tell you what you should do, but this is not a dress rehearsal. This is your actual life, right now. And you have no idea how long it's actually going to last. So if you are sitting there thinking: *What I really want to do is X,* honey, you better do it now.' But a lot of people say to me, 'What if I do XYZ and it doesn't work? How am I going to get back in?' " Women know that if we don't follow the form of the success model, we surely risk its contents and rewards.

Losing Our Identities

One of the reasons women don't leave work is for the simple, solid, and extremely valid reason that they love what they do. I loved being a publisher—deciding on books, shaping them, marketing them. I loved being a mentor, an advocate. I loved that when someone asked me what I did, I could tell them my title and they got it immediately. I loved not having to explain myself. But when women subvert the rest of their lives to their work identity, it makes it almost impossible to change anything because changing work would mean changing who they were. Susan Wittig Albert, author of *Work of Her Own,* observes that "without external credentials, I felt that my life had no meaning. Without the work that filled up my days, I was empty; I was not real," she recalls. "I had so fully defined myself in the context of my successful career that I had no other self."[3]

While she certainly represents an extreme, most working women understand how much of their identity they get from their work. This is true whether or not children and husbands are part of the equation. Forty years ago women looked to their roles as wives and mothers to identify them to the world. Now, instead of getting our identities from men or family, we get them from business cards, thus giving our professions an enormous psychic hold on our lives. Harvard economist and author Juliet Schor cites a time-use expert who observed, "We have become walking résumés. If you're not doing something, you're not creating and defining who you are."[4] Research shows that this is far from being a baby-boom phenomenon. Judging ourselves and other people by the work they do has become entrenched in Western culture as a laudable character trait.

While this heightened sense of a work identity reached its peak in the yuppie era, it's still very much a factor for women who have worked consistently for years. Most career women worked before they became lovers, partners, or parents. Yet most women admit that at a certain point, by virtue of the amount of time they spent at their work, they let slide other parts of their identities: hiker, gardener, cook, volunteer. Or the other parts of them became compartmentalized: "I am a mother from six P.M. to six A.M., and a wife on Wednesday nights when we have a baby-sitter. Other than that I'm a saleswoman," said Ellen McLeod, who works in the garment industry. "I guess it works, but I'm not terribly happy. I don't feel like I have a life anymore."

Sooner or later, though, in order to grow, the work identity needs to be placed in what eighty-year-old Zen priest Charlotte "Joko" Beck calls "a bigger container," which for many women is scary. Scary enough to stop us in our tracks. When we spend so many years becoming something, we fear we will become nothing. For commercial real estate saleswoman Marissa Clark "leaving my career was the most courageous thing I've ever done." She said she could make a career switch only when "it became clear to me that there was more to life than pursuing an identity so that I could be recognized by the world as valuable. For years my career fulfilled my sense of responsibility. Selling was easy. I had established myself and I had respect and I had status. I had a very good income and I had every reason to believe that this would be something that would be maintained for a sustained period of time." So why did she give all that up?

"Part of being in the business world felt like I belonged to something too. I felt like I belonged to the community of executives, the power brokers. I paid a price to belong to that world and part of the price I paid was to become almost predictable. To give up the established identity that had made me more comfortable seemed self-indulgent at first. But I knew that the external life that I had nicely set up for myself was limiting me. I found that there was a whole world within me that I had left undiscovered that was asking to be explored. There was a need to explore the universe within me as opposed to being settled in the universe outside me. I think I began to recognize there was a facade about

125

what I was doing. Even though everything appeared to roll off of me, my ability to put on my executive face was not effortless anymore. The facade now felt empty, is what happened."

Angels and Good Girls

There's another very sneaky part of this work identity that we are reluctant to give up. Since over the years we have been rewarded for being team players, "good girls," we have come to see these attributes as being a good part of who we are. And these attributes have no real value outside of a male system of success. Cut off from the system, there is no use for them and they wither and die. Healthy as that may be, it still represents a loss of self—false or otherwise. In a lecture Virginia Woolf gave in 1931 called "Professions for Women"[5] she talked about this phenomenon, which she called "The Angel in the House." Woolf discovered that if she were going to work truly and review books as she really wished, with integrity, she had to kill this phantom that slipped behind her and whispered, " 'My dear, you are a young woman. You are writing about a book that has been written by a man. Be sympathetic; be tender; flatter; deceive; use all the arts and wiles of our sex. Never let anybody guess that you have a mind of your own.' " Woolf's Angel instructed her about how to fit in and meet with society's approval. Perplexing questions, those that might challenge the male/female relationship, "according to the Angel in the House, cannot be dealt with freely and openly by women; they must charm, they must conciliate, they must—to put it bluntly—tell lies if they are to succeed."

Sixty years later women are no longer as tightly bound to the classically feminine. But the Angel is still the hero's handmaiden. The Angel has sat on my shoulders, directing me away from behavior that could jeopardize a social or professional position. I have offered myself as a vessel through which corporate policy was poured and not formed. Close to the end of my last job, as I was beginning to be ground down by all this, I received a phone call from an agent whose author was miserable. "He signed up to do a book with your publishing house," she explained. "Everyone who was there then is gone now. He's war weary and just wants to pay your company back. He doesn't even want to write a book now." As much sense as the argument made to me (and as much as I believed letting him go was the correct thing to do), I told the agent that the company wished to hold her client to his contract and he would not be released from his obligation. I didn't agree with the position personally, but it wasn't up to me. But if I'm very honest with myself, in the staff meetings that led to the refusal I fought for the author's position only to a point—I didn't want to jeopardize my relationship with management over someone whom I'd never met. I knew that if I had any hope of staying in my employer's good graces, I'd have to listen to the Angel inside me, be a good girl, and learn to keep quiet. I lost much of my self-respect in the process of upholding that position. That's one of the ironies of obeying the Angel—we are rewarded for compliant behavior even as it erodes our lives. Yet we are still reluctant to let go of the identity. We are attached to the recognition and sense of false belonging we think the Angel brings us. She keeps us attached to her and to our roles in our companies with the slender thread of imagined acceptance.

Of course a big part of the good-girl phenomenon is survival. As Dr. Lillian Rubin, author, therapist, and social scientist, points out, "Women are aware they are judged by a different standard, just as blacks are judged by a different standard. They are always walking a fine line by the kind of behavior they think is permitted to them. They can't be too confrontational, too aggressive, because that doesn't work." But an even larger part is a psychological contract. Since we know we aren't allowed to compete fully with the men as men, if we are good girls, if we are overly responsible, if we conciliate and agree, we will then get the recognition we need from our co-workers. It's as if women need the reinforcement that we are good people because we are model employees, paragons of self-sacrifice. "Corporate America loves overly responsible people like me," Ann, a producer, said. "They count on the fact that if it needs to be done, I will get it done. I've never left anything dangling in my life. At a certain level it doesn't feel *safe* for me to do that. I know I pride myself on being able to do it even though it has made me into a nervous wreck trying to get everything done on time. Because I'm afraid to say no, things have gotten out of control."

"The good-girl thing is big," says Shelly Lazarus, CEO of Ogilvy and Mather. "Women are afraid to be themselves. They are afraid to set boundaries. They are afraid to take control of their lives. They think I can do it because I'm a big shot now, I'm 'Shelly Lazarus,' but I've been Shelly Lazarus all my life and it never hurt me even when I was an assistant." Our perceptions are probably more distorted by this good girl/perfectionist phenomenon than anything else. Shelly Lazarus remembers that when she was young, she once watched a young media planner running around her boss's office. "She was literally going around in circles tearing at her hair because she had promised a client a media plan by one o'clock and the computers were down. My boss looked at her and said, 'Calm down. What are they going to do. Take your children?' " Lazarus often reminds people of that story. When we endow perfection with that urgency, we completely lose perspective on what is really important. Being a good girl masks our real relationship with our work as it imprisons us.

Joan Didion once observed that "it is possible for people to be the unconscious instruments of values they would strenuously reject on a conscious level." Nothing could be more true regarding good girls. The entire process is so silent and feels so natural after all the years of schooling and practice, we are unconscious that the force even operates in our lives. We don't see it because we have grown up with it. We don't see it because we accept it as part of the dues paid for accomplishment. We don't see it because on an unspoken level we feel we can't change it. But when we achieve success on these terms, the Angel lives another day.

The system rewards women who don't challenge it. One of the ironies of obeying the Angel is that we are rewarded for compliant behavior even as it erodes our lives. When we try and alter the traditional path of success, we stop being "good girls." When we stop being good girls, the rewards of success are jeopardized. We are afraid of being ostracized from the very system we want to be free of.

Perfectionism is the biggest expression of being a good girl. Like most women I know, I truly believed that if I just worked hard enough and got all the pieces right, if my work was above criticism, then I could make any job work for me. As long as I focused on being a citizen above suspicion, I couldn't question

129

the system that was judging me. This is a sneaky resistance. My perfectionism kept me tethered to my profession by my pride. Because pride is such a huge part of perfectionism, it's hard to talk about the good-girl role; it feels humiliating. But many women admit it's a big part of what motivates them. One woman said that when she performed less than perfectly she felt the world was going to open up and swallow her; error wasn't an option. It felt like her very survival was on the line. When we bring that kind of emotion into the picture, we can't see the real relationship clearly. And because of an equation of imperfection and exile, we often won't do anything—no matter how miserable we can get—that we feel would jeopardize our lives. When we endow perfection with that urgency, we completely lose perspective on what is really important. Being a good girl becomes as much a part of our identity as being successful.

Social Resistance

Most women feel the gravity pull of the work identity when it comes to social interaction. There's a powerful reason for this. As Albert said, "A successful woman who chooses to leave her career risks trading her work-enhanced identity for one that is worth a great deal less on the social-status market."[6] Juliet Schor, too, found in her early research and interviews on downshifting that women continued to identify themselves by their most recent professional position.

Susan Mercado is a thirty-eight-year-old attorney who decided to take a year off when she didn't make partner in a San Francisco law firm. "The first month I was shell-shocked, I think," she says. "Then I had a total identity crisis. I remember bumping into someone I went to law school with at the supermarket who asked me what I was up to. I must have spent fifteen minutes explaining that I was only taking a little time off and that I planned to do pro bono work and all this stuff. For Pete's sake, she only asked what I was doing. I could have said grocery shopping, I mean, I lost it!" On top of that Susan admits she was upset that she found herself apologizing for her life. "I knew there was nothing wrong with what I was doing. But I almost felt ashamed. My first response was to go home and make some phone calls about finding new work even though that was not at all what I wanted."

Schor found that fear of loss of acceptance in society was a huge motivator in keeping people from making changes. "When I lost my job," says Lauren, a thirty-five-year-old restaurant manager, "I couldn't afford the car payments anymore and had to give the car back. It was humiliating at first driving this heap I bought on the cheap. But it saved insurance money and freed up money for other things. It also meant I could have a little more time to figure out what I wanted to do. I was getting sick of working for other people and I wanted my own place, even a franchise, but I wasn't sure if I could swing it. The kids were so embarrassed, they asked me to drop them off around the corner from school. These aren't spoiled kids. But all their friends' mothers had Volvos and Explorers and here I am driving my I-couldn't-cope car. They got over it but it hurt me. I kept wondering if I had done the right thing for them."

Fear

Behind all the forces of resistance is fear. It is our most powerful adhesive. Juliet Schor found "there's a big fear of the unknown and fear of dropping out of something that is so ingrained and second nature. There's the whole social-embarrassment issue. That's very important even if it isn't articulated that much. People are afraid their middle-class lives and appearances may be put into jeopardy. That's a very powerful and good reason to be afraid."

The first way we know to fight fear is with evidence that we are doing the right thing, the quickest proof of which usually lies in the tangible rewards of money and things. Our first inclination when we get frightened is to circle back to the tried and true. We run for the safety of doing what we've been praised for in the past. We run for economic security. Breaking the cycle of fear requires three things: a vision of another way of living, the confident expectation that it can be done (a plan), and the support of family, friends, or a community. Given the scarcity of role models, the latter becomes crucial.

We're naturally afraid to risk letting go of our hard-won gains. We've invested so much of ourselves in our careers that risking them feels like putting our very selves in danger. Furthermore, we get angry that we are the ones who are asked to change, not the system. But in the face of a rigid system of working, life eventually forces us into triage. That's when we discover that we've been dependent on a system that isn't dependable. This naturally leaves us feeling naked, vulnerable. When we look at why we resist change, we are forced to look under our self-protecting armor and it's scary. A nun in Minneapolis recalls the time she was contemplating leaving her order. She likened herself to a lobster when it loses its shell. "I had to grow, but I had to shed my protection," she says, "but while I am defenseless, I know, like that lobster, I have to hug the reefs, stay low and out of the way."

We resist change for all these very good reasons. Having some fear of the unknown is sure proof of sanity. But then there is the overwhelming fear that keeps us in bad marriages, unhealthy relationships, and limiting work situations. That kind of fear tells us that we will not only lose our identities, our place in society, and the food on our tables, it tells us we will never be able to take another vacation, our children will not go to college, and we will never have meaningful work again. That manner of fear concludes that we should hold on to what we've got with all we've got—no matter what.

CHAPTER 6

The Importance of Money

ONE MORNING IN SEPTEMBER OF 1994, when my husband was in the bathroom shaving, I slid a twenty-dollar bill out of his billfold and stuffed it into the toe of my sneaker. Instantly horrified, I recognized the cringing, shameful feeling as the same one I used to get in junior high when I would pinch money from my dad to go to the movies or buy cigarettes. What I had done was completely against my principles and every sense of who I was. But my money fears were so powerful, they overruled all my moral safeguards.

I had been out of work for three months and was in a deep funk about what to do with the rest of my life. I was no longer earning money and with every penny I spent, I felt more deeply dug into emotional debt to my husband (who is a wonderful and supportive man but who had complex feelings of his own about this money thing). A few days earlier he had made a pretty innocent comment about the size and scope of the Visa bill. Overly sensitive, I immediately determined I would go on a starvation money diet. At least if I wasn't bringing any money in, I wouldn't let money out. Until that point I always had prided myself on the fact that I wasn't a woman who wanted lots of clothes or shoes or makeup or things. The only problem was, I wasn't realistic about what I actually needed. So, after finding what I thought would be a week's money gone after only five days, rather than face the reality of my spending structure, I put my hand in the till.

This story isn't about the need for cash. I could have gone to the bank and withdrawn more. What it's about is that I didn't want to face my spending habits and my new economic power-lessness. I had been self-supporting for twenty years in part so that I would never be in the position where someone could control my actions by controlling the money. My husband had married an economic partner, not a dependent. I had never had to think twice about buying a new lipstick or toys for my child. Now I felt I had to answer for every penny spent (I didn't—but I felt I did) and I didn't like it. Not one bit. I vowed I would begin looking for a new position immediately. I had run the gauntlet of identity crises, societal pressures, and rearranged personal expectations and ambitions only to slam into the brick wall of financial insecurity and loss of independence. That day I realized that the demon worries of dependence and financial insecurity could, even more than my principles, rule my life.

The eleventh *Money* magazine survey of people's attitudes about money shows I've got plenty of company in my slightly panicky feelings on the subject. The results emphatically demon-strate that women worry much more about money than do men. We even think about money more. We are more concerned about paying the bills, about low raises, about future financial security. We are even more preoccupied with money than with romance: 60 percent of women (versus 34 percent of men) think more about "dollars than dalliances," yet we admit to enjoying sex more. Funny as the example seems, it shows how strong a magnet money is. Our worries about having enough of it pull us away from the things we say we deeply value: balance, meaning, caring, and time for family, friends, and ourselves.

In a twenty-year perspective on women and money, the Virginia Slims Opinion Poll said that money is the chief source of stress and resentment in women's lives.[1] More than 80 percent of the women I surveyed said money was critical to their sense of independence, two thirds admitted they felt judged by the amount of money they made, and more than two thirds of the women said that money was important to their sense of well-being.

Yet if you ask women about money (which immediately becomes equated with materialism), they firmly state that money for money's sake isn't important to them. Actually, they go even farther: in a major study conducted by the Whirlpool Foundation, people complained that money—and materialism—is too important in our lives. People felt that "materialism, greed, and selfishness increasingly dominate American life, crowding out a more meaningful set of values centered on family, responsibility, and community. People express a strong desire for a greater sense of balance in their lives—not to repudiate material gain, but to bring it more into proportion with the nonmaterial rewards of life."

An uneasy polarity exists where money is concerned: we condemn it as crass materialism keeping us away from what we value, yet when it comes to doing something about it, we are stopped cold by fears of not having any or by the need to maintain our lifestyles. This is not a recipe for happiness. Indeed, this dynamic keeps us in imaginary chains, bound to work we don't like. It keeps us in relationships we don't want. It consumes time and energy we want for other activities. It keeps us from changing our lives. In 1995 a major study of women's work lives concluded that "the crucial obstacle to moving ahead with new priorities is simple but profound: we are deeply ambivalent about wealth and material gain. While we decry the crass materialism of our society and its consequences, we also want 'success' for ourselves and our children. Most people express strong ambivalence about making changes in their own lives. . . . They want to have financial security and live in material comfort, but their deepest aspirations are nonmaterial ones."[2] Thus the opposing forces are set up: most of us live in that gap between absolute need and perceived need. We have to be awfully miserable to take any action that jeopardizes our incomes.

The problem with addressing money is that it's like water. It's hard to get your hands on; it takes the shape of its container, but is itself invisible. We really see what money means to us only in terms of what it can buy. Some of those things are intangibles like freedom, independence, status in the community. But what we don't often focus on is that earning money exacts a price from us by taking away our time. Since the desire for balance has become one of women's premier concerns, we have to begin to look more deeply at the decisions we make every day. Because money decisions always, at some level, involve making a choice among need, desire, and time, when we choose money, we necessarily bump the other parts of our lives down a slot on the priority list.

We can't begin to have balance until we unmask the promises that money makes to us about who we will be, how we will live, and what we are worth. It's not surprising that we resist an accurate portrayal of our relationship with money; it's so important to our self-definition and survival that it's very threatening to examine it directly. When we do so, we often find that we hide things we desire under the skirts of "need."

In assessing financial need we have to get an accurate picture of what is necessity and what is desire. We must distinguish between what is a financial fear and what is a financial fact. Otherwise, we cede control over our lives to misperceptions and phantoms.

Defining Need

For some women money isn't up for discussion. As Katie Martin, a forty-five-year-old hospital administrator, said, "It's not an issue. I have to work. I'm not married and I don't see any husband coming my way anytime soon. My parents are old; I'm the only one who can support them. And I have to save for my old age too." Janet Kennedy, a recently divorced woman with two children, said, "I was always the main money-maker in the family. Actually, I think my husband started to think about leaving me when I told him I was burned out and wanted to take a year off. I think he freaked out when he was faced with admitting to himself how dependent he'd become on my career. The good news, at

139

least, is that my lifestyle didn't change much with the divorce; I had always made the money."

These women whose incomes are necessary to support themselves or their families have become the new providers. Fifty-five percent of the women in my survey—a percentage consistent with other research conducted recently in the United States—contributed more than 50 percent to the family income. In other countries this is not so, but in most of the Western world the rise of unemployment and the continued movement toward downsizing has meant that it's usually the men who lose their jobs. When that happens, the women go to work (at lower salaries) to make ends meet.

When the woman is the only or major provider, either for herself or for her family, then all sorts of career problems have to be placed on the back burner. The priorities are clear, the choices more limited by necessity. These women feel trapped by their responsibilities, but most have resigned themselves to the fact that they don't have much choice about the matter. Because survival is the primary issue and not lifestyle or questions of identity, the choices are clearer and women have less denial and lower expectations. Overall, the women who truly needed to work to support themselves and their families had more resolution (if not peace) about their situation than the women for whom it wasn't as clear.

Creeping Consumerism

The more elusive part of the money discussion, however, lies in how we define necessity. Most of us live and work not to support our basic survival needs but our lifestyle choices. "Once our basic human needs are taken care of, the effect of consumption on well-being gets tricky," says Juliet Schor. "How many of us thought the first car stereo a great luxury, and then, when it came time to buy a new car, considered it an absolute necessity? Or life before and after the microwave? There is no doubt that some purchases permanently enhance our lives. But how much of what we consume merely keeps us moving on a stationary treadmill?[3]

Our sense of what we need becomes distorted by the fact that we do have to pay the bills for what we want. We continually spend more than we make. Thus, debt keeps us in "need." And debt has continued to rise: the average household's credit card bill increased 33 percent from 1993 to 1996.[4] So the feeling of need remains constant even though what we need seems to keep escalating.

The average American consumes twice what she or he did forty years ago—a fact for every class of people. (This is true even in the face of the largest income gap between rich and poor since the 1930s Depression and the fact that the standard of living for the poorest class has declined markedly.)[5] Fifty years ago less than half the homes had electric refrigerators; now all homes do. We also have vacuum cleaners, radios, televisions, and microwaves.[6] The entire post–World War II Western world has moved to the drumbeat of the great American consumer dream. Within a matter of two decades what had been a struggle for survival has become a contest. One man from Texas said, "Keeping up with the Joneses is killing me."[7]

Consumerism is insidious, and as Schor observes, "women are much more tied in than men. They are more invested in participating in the consumer economy. My suspicion is it defines them more. They're the consumers in the economy and they have been for a long time. Starting from the day when housewives did all the buying—not that they had all the decision-making power, but women do a disproportionate amount of purchasing." We don't think about education and children's shoes as consuming, but it is.

With every little thing we purchase, we have to work a bit more to make the increased payments, and our ties to our work tighten incrementally. To pay for our lifestyles we are working longer than we did forty years ago.[8] Americans now work the equivalent of two months longer than their counterparts in Germany and France. It's not a surprise that as the material side of our life improves, we often find the quality of our life has lessened. We've gotten into a cycle of spend and earn and spend and earn and what we really have to show for it is a decrease in leisure time. After we've gone to the office and made the beds, we have just sixteen and a half hours of nonwork time a week. In fact, for the past twenty years, contrary to all projections, work time has increased for most people.

Valuing Time and Money

In my research the importance of making money was a relatively steady part of women's lives: 75 percent said they felt it was important to their lives both now and in the beginning of their careers. But the way women valued their time has changed dramatically. Where 60 percent of women felt having time for themselves was important at the beginning of their working lives, 90 percent felt it was important today. The importance of having balance showed a similar growth: 60 percent of women felt it was important when they began working, versus 93 percent today. Women rate lack of time highest on lists of stress factors, and exhaustion is the hallmark of the working woman. Each woman interviewed said she didn't have enough time for herself. The desire for balance is another way of saying women want more "free" time to offset "waged" time, or work.

But we don't assign the same value to "free" time as we do to "waged" time. Wendy felt bad about asking her husband to take her son for a few hours on Saturday mornings after she'd been home all week so she could go to an exercise class. "He works all week. I feel guilty doing something for myself." I ask her if she hired a baby-sitter, would that person be working? "Yes," she replied. "Then aren't you working too?" I wondered. "I never thought of it that way," she replied. "It doesn't feel like it because I'm not getting paid."

There are people who get paid to teach aerobics, mountain climbing, writing. Yet, when we take the time to pursue any one of those activities at a financial sacrifice to ourselves and our loved ones, we often feel guilty or self-indulgent. It is a testimonial to how much the culture around us, and we ourselves, resist giving up money for time.

One of the ways time begins to have a conscious value for us is when it becomes finite, either through age or illness. For Sheila, an accountant who experienced menopause at forty-four, "it was like a wake-up call. It was always mañana with me. Tomorrow I'll diet. Tomorrow I'll take up painting. Tomorrow, tomorrow, tomorrow. But there was always something too pressing that just had to be done the next day, so that tomorrow just never got around to happening. I remember coming out of the gynecologist's office thinking a huge chapter on my life was over, and it changed the way I felt about all the other parts of my life. I never had kids and now it was too late. I didn't want to say that about other things."

When Betsy was diagnosed with breast cancer, work went overnight from the biggest thing in her life to the sidelines. "I had been wanting to pull back but it kept sucking me in," she said. "I'm sorry I had to get cancer to feel I had permission to take long walks or just sit quietly in the middle of the day and have a cup of tea. It's a cliché, but I really did do the deathbed check, and work was taking up way too much of my time. I'm sure there's another way of weaning away from work that's less drastic than this way. Now that I'm back at work full-time, I want to hold on to this perspective. So far, it's helping me enjoy everything more."

Our appreciation for time comes with age, which makes sense. In the beginning of our careers, when we are still young and immortal, we're happy to devote almost all our waking hours to what we think is building a life for ourselves. What we don't see at the start is that it will become harder and harder, the more invested we are in our careers, to grab back some of those hours. When we need the hours most—during the first ten to fifteen years of our children's lives—we often find that we are at the peak of our careers. In the tougher work environment, we often fear for our jobs if we take the hours we need to take care of our loved ones. In a pinch we usually do what we are paid for. The waged time takes priority in our days even as the unwaged time does in our hearts.

Eventually, we become so bound by the hours we devote to work that it actually becomes difficult for many women to make a transition to any free time at all. Even taking a vacation becomes difficult. "The first five days of my vacation are spent alternating between detoxing and obsessing about work. Then I have two days of downtime. Then back to work," said Sarah, a media planner. We are so used to having our time "taken" that when we give ourselves the gift of it, we don't value it. "Long hours were a really macho thing," said Ellie. "The more hours you put in, the more important you were." No wonder it's hard to have free time. Jill, a real estate broker, was taking a walk in the afternoon on one of the first spring days. "Isn't it a beautiful day?" she asked. "We're cheating," said her husband. "Not me," said Jill, "—I finished my work for today." "It's cheating," her husband repeated, "but I'm enjoying it." Time away from work is "stolen," "taken." We play "hooky." By our speech and our daily practice we clearly value work time more than free time.

The process of making money literally consumes our time, leaving us starved for it. "We actually could have chosen the four-hour day," Juliet Schor observes. "Or a working year of six months. Or, *every worker in the United States could now be taking every other year off from work—with pay.* Incredible as it may sound, this is just the arithmetic of productivity growth in operation."[9] If this is true, what powerful forces resist this kind of freedom? The power of the consumer culture, she answers. The ultimate resistance to changing our lives is that we value our money more than our time.

"Most people can cut twenty percent of their expenses and maintain their lifestyles," states Schor, which would translate into a four-day workweek. In fact, according to a study on women and economic security, 58 percent of women preferred work with just those kinds of flexible hours.[10] While corporate resistance to an altered work schedule remains the principal obstacle to a four-day week, Schor notes that there are real value dimensions to not reducing hours and wages. People fear they won't be taken as seriously. But as Schor points out, "consumerism is also a very strong inhibiting factor for change."

Dr. Lillian Rubin says she sees women all the time who say they would be glad to give up money for a better life. "Many of them are women in families with two good earners," Rubin notes. "But what stops them is that they have a lifestyle that requires that kind of money. And they aren't willing to give up the lifestyle. Whether it's going out to dinner or a movie, having nannies for the kids, having the best schools in the area, or a car phone where they can be in touch. It's all become necessary to them and they can't imagine life otherwise."

Dr. Rubin sees how this creeping consumerism has affected women. "I don't think psychology grows in a vacuum. It grows in a social cultural setting," she observes. She sees people in her research and among her friends who are "the yuppie types and they are in a panic about their five-year-olds. They are all convinced they are not going to have the options we had. If you really live that fear—and people do now—it begins to dominate your life. I tell people they are giving away their lives for something that may never happen and that their lives are totally bereft of any kind of meaningful time. And they turn to me and say,

'But everybody else is doing it.' '' With that kind of fear leading the way, people willingly forfeit time for money. The consequences of that decision (which masquerades as need, not option) are profound. We have become literally starved for time. Women are exhausted. Women with no families to support work longer hours to pay for enjoyable lives: health clubs, vacations, nice homes, and setting aside money for their retirement. But the time impoverishment is clearest with working mothers.

Research shows that women will spend anything and everything for the sake of their children. This urge, however, can end up locking them into a horrible cycle that robs them of all of what is laughingly known as free time. When questioned, most women say they don't see their desire to provide "the best" for their children and their time impoverishment in the same landscape. "Need" stands between the two, shielding and hiding the consuming connection. Yet they are linked, locked together in what Rubin says are fears and expectations: fears that their kids won't have all the opportunities, and expectations that if we work hard enough, we can provide them with everything they might need.

The result of this dynamic is a world of women stretched to the breaking point. "Every professional woman I know in her late thirties or early forties with young children has two sets of competing urgencies," Dr. Rubin says. "It's not just values, but *urgencies*. These women want and need a professional outside-the-home identity and they want and need an identity as a mother. These women are always caught. It's a zero-sum game. You only have so many hours in the day and so much energy, and the child is only awake so many hours. If you go to work at nine and come

147

home at six, there isn't that much time with a child." Rubin says she sees women frantic, men frantic, families frantic. "People feel their lives are on a merry-go-round. The men are working forty, fifty, sixty hours a week. They want to be fathers, not like their fathers were, and it's hard to do that at nine at night. Little kids stay up until ten, which leaves them tired, which leaves no couple time, no friendship time, and no time to catch up on the work you didn't do at the office." Very often the pursuit of a good lifestyle and the best for children makes the very thing it strives to serve impossible, leaving people depressed, breathless, and lonely (but with very good schools and cars). Until people are willing to push back the fear and consider sending their children to a school that might not cost so much, women and men stay chained by consumerism to a time clock they can't control. The hours sweep by in direct proportion to the numbers on the credit card bill.

The Promises Money Makes

If money meant only keeping up appearances, or wanting good schools, new microwaves, and car stereos, then it wouldn't be such a loaded issue. But wanting money has a lot to do with fighting fear. "Women are terrified of becoming bag ladies," says Kathleen Boyle, a financial planner specializing in women's investments. "It's their biggest fear. They just want to know they are going to be safe, safe, safe." Having money promises to keep those looming fears from coming true. Women won't be homeless, unable to care for themselves, without standing in the community. With money, women's children will never be embarrassed or want for anything.

For women, having money means survival, control, and freedom. It tells us and the world if we are successful or not. Money buys security. Money makes up for the indignities and injustices suffered in the male-dominated corporate environment. Far from being a matter of comfort or luxury, money means never having to be in the dependent box on someone else's tax form.

While it is inarguably true that we all need money to live and most of us want recognition from our friends, family and co-workers, the problem arises when we allow one thing—money—to give us so much power to alleviate our lives' problems. By our doing so, money becomes so important that we have no choice but to value it above all else, and by extension we value what we have to do to earn it too. Thus we end up in a weird bind: we need the money (we think) for our very material and psychological existence, yet we increasingly can't bear the values of the places we have to go to earn it.

The Promise of Independence

"Economic dependency brings emotional dependency—it's almost inevitable," says Lillian Rubin. Avoiding that state of existence propelled the women into the work world out of material and psychological necessity. Above all but absolute need, women prize their independence. Rubin herself remembers that when she first was married and a graduate student, she was economically dependent on her husband. "I know that for the first years of my marriage to Hank I was a student. Hank worked and supported us," she remembers. "Even things like buying him a gift were tough and in this life he would never have said, 'You can't spend money.' He felt it was ours and that we had enough. But there was no question in my mind that the money was his."

When Rubin became a professional and started making money, she felt profoundly better. "I know deep in my soul what the difference is," she says. "I know that I wouldn't have taken five hundred or a thousand dollars and spent it without feeling as if I should check it out, get Hank's permission. Now, if I wanted to spend five thousand I would do it. I would tell him, but I wouldn't ask, I wouldn't be checking anything out. And I would feel different about it and I do feel different about it."

Earning money gives women power and freedom and an independent identity apart from a man or family. That earning capacity is the block from which self-esteem, a sense of purpose, and personal freedom are carved. Women repeatedly said they wanted careers in large measure because they didn't want anybody dictating the terms of their lives for them.

Yet over time this purity of independence can become clouded. We make tiny decisions that incrementally create a way of living that handcuffs us to our paychecks. We don't see the chains that hang around us, connecting dreams to paycheck stubs. Many women admitted that they felt their desires had become hostages to money. Karen is a thirty-two-year-old single woman who supports her ailing mother. She has also just broken off an engagement to a man on whom she might have been able to depend economically. She voluntarily "stopped out" of her banking work for six months to recover from job burnout and to explore her dream of writing novels. But when her savings were depleted, she knew she had to go back to work. She really disliked banking and called me, wanting to know if she could make good money in publishing—which she thought she would enjoy more. Instead of immediately saying no—which would have been accurate—I asked her how important money was to her. "Extremely important," she said. "I've been poor and I don't want to go back there. I don't want to be cold. I don't want to be afraid I can't buy a plane ticket to see my folks, and I don't want ever to be yelled at by a shop clerk and not be able to turn on my heel, walk out, and shop somewhere else."

I told Karen how much money publishing paid. "I better go back to banking," she said. "I can't be poor and happy. I don't have it in me to start over. I'd rather be bored at my job and have a good income." Emotionally, Karen needed the security and freedom having money provides. Her need for independence was so profound and powerful, so much about psychological survival, that even though making it precluded other meaningful options in her life, she was willing to make that trade-off. Because Karen, like so many of us, needed money to ensure emotional independence, she had to face the unhappy reality that freedom was paid for with the time she wanted to spend on other things.

Consultant Janet Andre observes that sometimes the search for independence actually lands us in the same power relationships with work that we sought to escape through it. "Economic freedom is the core of everything in this country, and every country. It's what keeps women in jobs they don't like and in bad relationships. One of the reasons women hold on to their careers is that the jobs become almost too important because we have given up so much to get them. To me it was never the job, it was the

151

freedom of movement and not having to pretend and not having to be a subservient person. But, ironically, this is what happened to me at work. And the higher up I got, the more it happened." Many women told stories like Janet's: they fought to be free of the control or censure of fathers or mates only to find themselves in twisted economic relationships with their offices.

For many of us our very identities depend on being able to support ourselves. Jane recalls that the "two most difficult periods of my life independencewise were not when I got married, but when my soon-to-be husband, Alex, moved into this apartment and, more difficult by far, depending on him financially (even for a little while). I had worked my whole life. Until I was forty-five we had separate money," she says with visible unease. "I had my money. He had his. I had my bank account and he had his. Then, when we left our jobs and the stream of income stopped, it suddenly made no sense to continue to do that. We had what we had. And what we had was income from Alex's severance package and from our investments. We needed to reorganize everything. We had our first joint account, which was totally frightening. I got a credit card under his name. He managed the money. I felt like the earth slipped out from under my feet. He's a very generous man. It's not like he's controlling, but suddenly I wasn't earning money anymore. The money was a big piece of my independent identity."

Most women up and down the income scale feel as Jane does—that they need an independent income for the sake of their very identities. Only one third of the women in my research said that they would be comfortable depending on someone else for money if they stopped working for a while. Only 5 percent of the women said that money was unimportant to their sense of independence. Of all the statistics in the study that was the most bald.

Economic freedom may be a core part of our identities, but it also gives women power. Money and power go together. "There is nothing like money to be an equalizer," says Dr. Rubin. "When you are talking about women who are making decent money, they have a sense of power. They may come into my office and look totally powerless—especially if they are in that stage where they are panicked about not having a man or a baby—but what keeps them at work is the knowledge that without it they would really feel like nothing. They have the wherewithal to provide a very good life for themselves."

Money and Success

The most common measure of success we use is how much money a person makes. When people say, "Oh, she's really successful," they mean, "She's got lots of money." Power and status come from money. When we start to look at our relationship with money, one of the resistances is the fear that we will stop being successful if we trade money for time, or take a job that pays less well that we may enjoy more. In the male success model the more money you make, the more valuable you are. In a quest for value women, too, have adopted this measurement. As long as women are competing for equality, money is the scorecard of where we stand in the game. Yet it only measures a sliver of who we are.

A successful social status is heavily linked to money. When

Juliet Schor interviewed potential downshifters about their economic concerns, she found that the biggest blocks to change were not fears just about economic security but about social embarrassment. Schor found people were afraid that if they suffered a loss in income, their ability to keep up middle-class appearances might be put into jeopardy. "That's a powerful and good reason to keep working."

We don't sit down and quantify the appearances too often. Alison, who wants to set up her own business but doesn't feel she can afford it right now, admits she could be driving an older car. Yet, she doesn't want to be out of place in her new community. She focuses on the need for the car payment, but not the day a week she might be working to make it. As much as we may joke about it, keeping up appearances is still very important to our sense of self. At a party for a three-year-old one mother said she felt ashamed of her little five-dollar finger puppets when she saw the elaborate gifts the other mothers brought. When it was pointed out that the kid didn't know the difference between a five-dollar present and a fifty-dollar present, the mother replied, "She doesn't, but her mother does."

To an enormous degree social position depends on financial success. Income brackets have replaced the class system. People with no more than dollar signs to recommend them regularly fill the pages of magazines that are devoted to celebrating just those people. Our entire society has come to venerate success on such a level that we often overlook what we give up in order to ensure we don't jeopardize our income stream. Lillian Rubin recalls a client in her early forties who came to Rubin utterly depressed and bereft. This woman had been making more than a million dollars a year, yet she said that all she wanted to do was conceive a child. But she resisted cutting down on her work. The combination of her busy travel schedule and her husband's ambivalence almost ensured no baby was forthcoming. "You have to realize," Dr. Rubin said, "that even though women don't think they have made a choice, by the time they are in their late thirties or early forties, they have made a thousand choices that have led them to where they are. This woman wouldn't admit it, but her success and the money she made was more important to her than her desire to be a mother."

If the promises of having money whisper loudly enough, we lose all perspective on how much money is enough money. In interviews with women who had been through the high times in the 1980s in the financial community, this was extremely apparent. "No matter how much money you made, someone else was always more successful. It kept you going, it seemed that the barre was always being raised. Yet, if I compare myself to my sister, who's a nurse, I'm off the charts," said JoAnn Peletier, a forty-five-year-old former stockbroker. Like Ellie, JoAnn thought she was successful until she looked around at others. "It's relative," she says. "Today I am redefining what success means for me. But I had to go through the mill and out the other side before I could do that. I had to go to success hell and come back." If we allow money to be the chief measure of success, we will always find ways to be insufficient. Anchoring our value and our happiness to what money can buy is a dangerous move. It chains us to our paychecks and promotions and devalues the rest of our lives by default.

Showdown at Value Gap

Success, power, and independence are critically important to most working women. Good schools, good food, nice clothes, good music, beautiful homes, usually end up on the "most important" list as well. These things are important to men too. But since women's lives tend to be more multidimensional than men's—because of the responsibility of family—to have all these things we end up trading more of who we are than men do. From their earliest moments men are told their work is to chase that holy trinity—money, power, and success. They learn to value money and what it brings as a measure of their very manliness. Besides, they know that they really have little option: the Western world values men who value money and value men who make money. For women, however, it's less clear. Our relationship to money is historically more indirect: we had to attract and keep a man to have any. For many this is still true. As Gloria Steinem put it, "The economic power of an eighteen-year-old girl probably outweighs that of an eighteen-year-old boy because she has youth and beauty to trade for the man's currency. A lousy bargain, because fifty dollars you earn is better than five hundred dollars that make you dependent." We've come to value youth and beauty not only for themselves but for their earning power.

Since our work worlds are structured to best help men achieve what society thinks men should achieve, is it any surprise that when women go to work in those environments, they find themselves institutionally trapped between two different ways of valuing themselves and their lives? In the previous generations there was no value gap—just two separate worlds. But now, as the two worlds combine (as they have increasingly for both sexes), we have internalized the chasm that used to separate the two worlds. In my survey there were large gaps between how women spent their time and what they said they valued most. In every case there are circumstances that explain the gap, and in every case the circumstances always came down to the need for more money.

Our final and most difficult attachment to our work, then, is money. We think that if we make enough of it, if we have enough economic security, then we can tackle the problems of balance in our lives. Of course the fallacy in that thinking is that as long as we put money first, we continue to cement ourselves into the success system that creates the lack of balance in the first place. As Shelly Lazarus said, "God help you if you work and don't like what you are doing. Because no amount of money is going to make you happy. It just doesn't work that way."

The Cost of Money

We are paying for this money with our peace of mind. In a revealing snapshot the Virginia Slims Poll found that the most stressed people in America were women who were employed full-time and had kids under the age of thirteen. One percentage point below those women (and intersecting with them) were women who identified themselves as executives or professionals. Over the past twenty years 89 percent of women felt that the kinds of jobs open to them had improved, as had the compensation (86 percent) and the opportunities for leadership (86 percent). Yet 45 percent of women felt their marriages had gotten worse, and every study shows that working mothers fear their kids are affected by their mothers' lack of time. It's conditions like these that set up the tensions that send women rocketing out of the career orbit with lives out of control.

Even though most women believe that more money would make their lives easier, when they were asked in my survey what they want out of their lives, the answers are almost universally nonmaterialistic. Caring, connection, more time (and that old favorite, weight loss) were most often mentioned when women were asked what would make their lives and their world a better place. In fact, the 1995 study, *Yearning for Balance,* found striking results: "Nonmaterial aspirations consistently outranked material ones by huge margins . . . a majority of Americans would be much more satisfied if they were able to have more time with family and friends . . . if there were less stress in their lives, and if they were doing more to make a difference in their commu- nity."[11] The authors of the study were struck by the fact that people valued things to do with family and human connections rather than material achievement. When they asked the question "What prevents people from satisfying these [nonmaterial] aspira- tions? What is keeping them away from family and friends, and causing stress in their lives?" the answer was clear: Trying to keep up or to get ahead.

When asked if they would trade money for time, women all said yes with a huge *but:* they knew they would be trading more than money. They would be trading their aspirations and accom- plishments as well. Juliet Schor points out that making the income trade-off means "that people have to basically reject the standard model of success. If we are talking about professional and managerial women, because the work norms are such that you don't really don't have a lot of flexibility to work limited numbers of hours and still be a career and financial success, if you want to get balance in your life, you want to get time, you don't want to get put into one of those pigeonholes and you want to be a proper mother and have a career, chances are you are either going to have to make a career or big job change because most people have a lot of difficulty changing hours within their jobs. People switch to careers where they can get more balance or they drop out of the labor force altogether or they go into dead-end traps in their own occupation."

Given that the majority of women want to work, that careers provide much more than money—self-esteem, expression, independence, and identity—it looks like women are deadlocked between two value systems whose conflicts create stress and breakdown. It is very hard to learn how to revalue things in our lives that had no value before.

Women have struggled for economic equality, and the fact that they have to literally pay for it with the quality of the rest of their lives should be infuriating. The fact that too few women seem to be loudly complaining really scares Gloria Steinem because, as she points out, it means that many women have "bought into the idea that somehow they just weren't good enough." Rather than critique the values and behavior urged by our success culture, women take the blame for shortfalls in their expectations onto their own shoulders. "The culture is so busy trying to blame the individual and saying, 'Well, if you can't do it all, it's your fault,' " says Steinem with anger. "We just can't buy it, because then it makes women feel at fault. They ask, 'How come I'm not superwoman?' Well, no one is superwoman. It's not possible to do everything women think they should be doing. You cannot do it all without transforming the work structure," she emphasizes. "We can't integrate into the work structure as it is. There is no such thing as integrating women equally into the economy as it exists, it's not possible. Not with all the other responsibilities women have. Not until the men are as equal inside the house as women are outside it. Not until we transform the system."

As work is structured, we are forced to make a choice. What is going to come first? If it's money, then we have to understand that it won't do all the things it promises to do. We can't begin to make changes in our lives that align us with what we say we want until we honestly scrutinize the value and the priority we place on these promises. Until we do so, we will continue to live in the gap between what we say we want and what we actually do. "It means reordering your values," says Lillian Rubin. She's right. We will be unable to make any changes in our lives until we fully face what money means to us.

CHAPTER 7

Changing

I AM NO DIFFERENT FROM OTHER WOMEN:
I make changes in my life out of disgust or desire. The way I make
changes, however, more often resembles an exercise in triage
rather than one of choice. I only make the big moves when it's
abundantly clear that something *must* be done. Unless my very
sanity is at stake, I'll find some way to hold on to what is weighing
me down because I think that's the right thing to do. I'm a good
girl.

I'd been bumping along what felt like the bottom of a well
for a few months in my new job when I went to see a counselor.
Expecting some advice about weighing the pros and cons, I was
surprised when, instead, she told me a story about a woman
swimming across a lake with a rock in her hand. As this woman
neared the center of the lake, she started to sink from the weight
of the stone. "Drop the rock," shouted some people who were
watching from the shore. But the woman kept swimming, now
disappearing for moments at a time under the water. "Drop the

rock!" the onlookers hollered louder. The woman had reached
the middle of the lake and was now sinking as much as she was
swimming. Once more the people urged, "Drop the rock!" And
as the woman disappeared from sight for the last time, they heard
her say, "I can't. It's mine."

I hated that story. But I got the message: In order for my life
to lighten up, I was going to have to let go of what was weighing
me down. I was looking to my career to give me more than it
possibly could provide. Between the changes in the corporate
climate over the course of my career and the expectations I placed
on my work to define my existence (if not reward my soul), I had
just loaded too much on something that could no longer bear the
weight. And when my career stopped giving me the recognition
or satisfaction I depended on, well, I found that I had very little
else to rely on for my self-worth and identity. Of course I didn't.
For twenty years I'd spent most of my waking hours focused on
very little else.

I'd lived long enough to know that I'd made two kinds of
changes in the past—surface ones and deep shifts in perspective.
Without the latter I'd found the first kind rarely ended up enduring. If I wanted to make a lasting change, the time had come for
me to drop the rock. I had to drop the rock of my fear of not
having enough money. Drop the rock of my great expectations of
doing it all and doing it all well. If my career hadn't been on the
line, I wouldn't have paid such deep attention to the fact that I
was all out of whack. But I had hit the sink-or-swim point. I was
finally willing to let go of those ultimately unrealistic pictures I
had for my life and for my work. I was going to have to start to
define success for myself.

Triggering Change

I knew what the options were: I could continue as I was—unhappy, but highly employed. Having jump-started my attitude over and over, however, I was pretty sure that my battery just wouldn't hold the charge. I could switch jobs (which I'd done three times in the previous six years) but nothing looked better than where I was. Or I could really take a risk and stop work for a while and get a handle on what to do with my life. Since I was reluctant to make another change that might not work, I screwed up my courage and took a step into the unknown.

It happens that I chose to leave. But most women usually need some external event to give them permission to do something else with their lives. "It's very hard to pull your own trigger," says consultant Janet Andre, referring to whatever catalyst finally shakes a woman sufficiently to bring about change. "What I admired about Ellie Daniels was that she was able to pull her own trigger without an external excuse. Most of us need some kind of reason, 'I just had kids, I just got married, my mother's sick,' whatever. It's usually a family-related thing. Very rarely do you see people who say, 'I don't want to do this anymore because this is not who I want to be.' " For me the trigger was a change in management; for Jane it was the changing corporate climate.

Overall, women said that they left or changed their work either because they lost their jobs or because it was impossible to balance everything when their jobs grew more and more demanding. This is especially true during certain time periods in women's lives. With the combination of little work flexibility and higher expectations (because we are women), we have to work

163

harder and better for our success, which makes it nearly impossible to stick it out when demands outside of work increase. Janet Andre found that "only the most organized, together, talented women were able to make it through that gauntlet of childbearing and husbands and family stuff and all the demands of work." The other reason women left their jobs, Andre observed, "was because even if they were able to hang in there, they weren't going to get the job anyway. So, even if you were willing to sacrifice yourself on this altar of executive dream, the chances of your getting the job against a less qualified, less committed, but more appealing man because of his gender and his ability to fit in and be one of the boys is so great that a lot of women don't think it was worth it. So they went into other jobs. I did an alumni survey [for a major financial institution that had lost eighty percent of their female talent at a point when they were most productive], and it showed that more than ninety percent of the women who left were still working. It shocked them." Women weren't leaving work to be at home; they were leaving to continue working more sanely.

In Rosabeth Moss Kanter's research she found that as women's opportunities lessen, dissatisfaction increases. Thus, women become readier to make a change when the rewards for their current efforts diminish steadily and demonstrably. Because many women have families by the time the advancements slow or stop, it becomes simple for people to say that those women have stopped their work or changed what they do because of family commitments.

Yet in interview after interview, when the surface was scratched, women admitted that yes, they wanted more flexibility and time for their children, but if they had been happier in their work, they would have figured it out somehow. Work was too important to them economically and too important to their identities to leave altogether. Besides, every woman I talked to wanted to work. My research shows that if financial concerns weren't an issue, less than ten percent of the career women studied would be full-time mothers. When first interviewed, Alicia Daymans said she decided to leave her position because she wanted to spend more time with her daughter. Yet, after prolonged discussion, the real reason surfaced: she had real moral and philosophical differences with the magazine's owners. Certainly spending time with her preadolescent daughter was a big concern, but she admits that alone wouldn't have prompted a radical change in her employment.

Alicia agonized about her situation for a while but it was something from left field that actually triggered the change. "This is going to sound weird," she confessed, "but my daughter wanted to go to Sunday school and we ended up going to a Methodist church a friend of hers went to because I wasn't religious. In order to take her to Sunday school, I had to sit through the service. Suddenly, I had an hour every week to sit and think." Being in an environment where people were doing socially responsible work gave her the courage to find a job where she could work four days a week and explore a dream to go back into teaching as well.

But for other women "what usually happens is there is an event that triggers change," says Shoya Zichy, many of whose clients come to her at this point. "They are downsized. One of the things that happens when you are unhappy is that it communicates itself in very subtle ways. You don't work as many hours, you're not quite as eager a beaver, so that can effectively begin to show. You become a candidate for downsizing."

Age becomes a real factor in pulling the trigger as well. If it isn't the health of those around us, as in Jane's experience, our own mortality can be a real catalyst for change. For Donna, an IBM executive, only a grave illness stopped her in her tracks long enough to get some perspective on her life. "All I did was work from seven A.M. to midnight every day. I worked through the weekends. I knew I was on scary territory. There was a part of me that felt I had to do this because I didn't want anyone to badmouth me and say I couldn't do it. The inability to say no and take care of myself brought me to my knees. It was like being a captive and buying in and I didn't have the energy to change. I got so wrapped up and I was so cut off from other measures of what is normal. It was like going down a chute and not knowing how to stop myself and waiting for someone to stop me. It was worse than getting cancer, because I knew I was on a slide into hell and I didn't know where the bottom was."

One day Donna discovered a lump in her breast. "When I found out I had cancer, I kept working as if nothing was happening for three days. After three days I realized, *I can't do this.* And then I literally unclicked. Just like that, the most important thing in my life was to get well and I dropped work like a hot potato. I had no second thoughts about it. Whammo—I had an independent identity. I was so clear on my goals to get well and to live life to the fullest every day. One of the things I said to myself was, *I could put my life on hold for a year because I had to go through a year of chemo, but what if, at the end of the year, I'm dead? What if I don't make it? Then this will have been the only year of my life left. I think I better really have a great time.* So I used work to anchor me. I did only what made me feel good. I eliminated everyone in my life who didn't make me feel good. It was the most intense year of my life and I never regretted it."

Donna tried to reestablish herself at work after her year of chemo but she couldn't get interested in it, so she took a leave of absence. "It was the scariest thing I ever did. It was tough times at IBM and I knew they were laying people off, but I just had to do it." Donna got married during her leave, and at the end she took a buyout when it was offered. "I wouldn't have taken it if I hadn't had cancer," she said. "I could see what was happening at IBM and I said to myself, *Do I want that kind of pressure?* I was very glad I took the buyout. It was amazing. I remember signing the papers and saying to my boss, 'This is a big fucking deal.' "

Change Involves Mourning

At fifty-five the last thing Robin Ingram expected was to be fired. With relief she had just signed a new contract at her company, where she had been the director of corporate communications for more than twenty years. Robin assumed that she would coast through the last three years of her career. But when a new president was named six months into Robin's contract, she found herself swept out of her life's profession because she was too closely associated with the former administration. "I always used to joke that corporations were the tool of the devil," she says, "but I never thought that applied to me. I had seen the way others were treated, but I had escaped somehow. Now it's my turn. I'm alternating between depressed and furious."

I tell Robin that it took me a good year before I felt back on my feet after I left my job. I still have occasional nightmares about being fired (I had been laid off twice before because of acquisitions and mergers). Even though leaving this time had been my decision, I was no more than a few steps out of the exit door when I discovered I had a lot of mourning to do. I had to say good-bye to more than just the job, I had to change the whole way I lived my life. The checklist of things to be accomplished had kept me occupied. The busy calendar proved to me that I was needed and liked. The money meant I hadn't had to sweat every purchase, and the title on my business card made me an excellent person to introduce at a dinner party. I had to mourn the loss of the very real community I had been part of day in and day out. Mostly, though, I had to mourn the loss of my dream life—the one that would come about if only . . .

The hardest part about my intense grief was suddenly feeling that I, alone without my work to go to every day, was simply not enough. I came nose-to-nose with my dependency on something over which I ultimately had no control—my career. I saw how much power I drew from it, and when the source of supply was removed, I went dark inside. In many emotional ways I wasn't so different from the mothers of friends of mine who found themselves without identity or purpose when their husbands of thirty years gave them the heave-ho to marry other (usually younger) women. Some of those women got stuck in their mourning. Others got up, shook themselves off, and created new lives that were much richer than the old ones.

168

Grief has a big role in change. It helps us learn from and let go of the past. In mourning something we take stock. In the case of work we see where it filled us up and emptied us out. If we don't go through the grief process, we won't be able to move on emotionally. In all my interviews I've yet to meet a woman who lost her job or voluntarily left it who wanted to return to the work world under the same conditions. They all said that what happened to them helped them to see clearly that they had depended on something inherently undependable. They might be looking forward to a new intellectual or creative challenge in their new work, or a better pay package or a job with more meaning, but they sure weren't going back with the old expectations of being taken care of, no less recognized or praised. They were going to work to do the work. Nothing more. Nothing less.

This was certainly true of Petra Baker, who found herself faced with the option of either taking a lower-level job (with the same pay) at her technology company or leaving altogether when her company restructured. Adding to the sting of losing her position, Petra felt betrayed by her boss and mentor, the new CEO of the company. She felt she had gone overnight from being his protégée to being his whipping girl. It was only when Petra began to accept what was happening that she felt some control come back into the situation. She saw that while what had happened was beyond her control, how she chose to deal with it wasn't. She couldn't afford to leave, so she took the offered position. But her expectations were much different about work after that. She separated who she was from what she did and several months later, she says she feels better about her work and herself. She's even managed to find some things she likes about her new job more than the old one—a creative community, some stimulating work. She feels so much less invested in pleasing everyone and being perfect that she is actually enjoying work again. Like Petra, it's often only when we are forced to let go of something that we can clearly see the problems. It's only when we come to that point that we become willing to change our agendas and perspectives.

Balance

I want what most women want—a good mix of work, play, love, and meaning. I want balance. But I had been so focused on the more measurable things in my life—money and success—I had neglected the inner, less quantifiable parts of my life. Shoya Zichy suggests to her clients that they think about rebuilding their lives the way a potter constructs a pot. "You have an inner hand and an outer hand," she says, "and it is keeping the pressure constant between them that creates that pot. The outer hand is all the factors of genetics and intelligence and family support, expectations, education, and opportunities in life. If you have judged your whole life by how the outer hand is doing, the pot collapses on itself; that's what burnout is. The inner hand is the innate, inborn psychological type that dictates your preferences, what releases the most energy in you. That's the one that we don't have a handle on." Zichy, who has seen hundreds of women move to a place of balance, concludes, "Once you see what you really have to do and want to do, you aren't afraid of it. It's not that you can do it overnight, but if you have a sense of direction about where you're going, then all of a sudden you wake up in the morning and say, 'I'm in control again.' "

The answer to making work and life enjoyable and fulfilling lies in using the two separate forces in a balanced way so that they combine to form a whole. We weren't too far off in our original expectations for life—a whole life does combine work and personal life. It just does it without the overlay of the success culture, the consumer mind-set, and the business-card identity. "Too much emphasis on the outer hand, and you have lost control of that pot," Zichy says. "It's when you start to trust the inner hand that you regain balance and control." But trusting this "inner hand" means moving away from the male success model's gold standard of what is valuable: accomplishment, power, and money. It means relying on an internal sense of what is important to each person; it means putting a value on friendship and family and time that is equal to the value of success. It means changing the contents and order of the success checklist and timetable. It means bringing the private into the public world. And, doing this feels like risking an entire culture's recognition and approval.

As with the women in my research, over the years I'd been working, the importance of ambition, money, position, and power had dwindled. Instead, friendship, family life, having fun and independence, became more important. Yet, it was precisely those things that the majority of the women said they had no time to enjoy. Their outer lives were dictating the amount of space the inner life occupied. And as the jobs became more demanding, the inner space got smaller and smaller and smaller.

To have full lives we have to bring our inner and outer lives into balance. This means we have to learn to value ourselves for who we are, not for what we do. As Anna Quindlen said, "You have to get strong enough to let your values override the values of the culture and the values of the corporation. You get strong enough to say, 'Yeah, I know how the world defines success. But, you know, I'm too old and too smart and too accomplished to let anybody define success for me but myself.'"

Reclaiming Ourselves

It would be nice if change could happen neatly and sequentially—first we change our perspective and then we change our actions. For most of us, however, it doesn't work that way. Instead, as we stumble around in the dark, we find we're in the middle of a messy process of weighing the external and the internal, the concrete and the amorphous, the proven and the risky. At four o'clock in the morning we know exactly what to do with our lives. And three hours later this certainty dries up and disappears along with the evening stars.

May Benson found herself in just this position a few years ago. Her story typifies the struggle of women who want to reclaim who they are and what is important to them. Defined by what she did but wanting a life that included balance, meaning, and quality, May thought she had found a way to integrate the two worlds. Yet, as it turned out, she had to ultimately reject both to forge something new.

Like most of the women interviewed, May, who graduated college in the mid-seventies, just "assumed I was going to work. I assumed that at some point I was going to get married; and I assumed I would stay working after I had kids and I assumed I would have kids. Because I was brought up to think that I could do all that. I wanted a career but I didn't have an image of what that was. My first career goal was to be a psychotherapist, but I quickly realized that if I wanted to do anything significant in that field, I was going to have to get a Ph.D. and not a master's, and I couldn't go to school any longer."

May ended up following a boyfriend to Seattle. "I looked for one of those proverbial jobs that was challenging, interesting, well paying. It almost didn't matter what the title was as long as it met the other criteria." May found that work hard to come by, so she worked temporarily at a department store. Five years later she was the buyer for its biggest department. Six years later, bored and "plateaued" May decided to get an MBA. "I'd always been pretty good at math and business, so I figured, why not? It was never something that I really thought about. I did a lot of self-evaluation, but I was clearly swept along with the fact it was the early eighties, and I had fun with it and it felt right at the time."

After business school May spent ten years doing corporate lending work, moving up very nicely through the ranks. She married a co-worker ("We both stayed in the company, but he switched departments. You end up working so hard in those jobs that the guys at work are the only ones you get to know") and became the first female managing director in her department. Eight years into work she became pregnant with her first child. "I thought, *This is kind of cool. I've got to start talking to people and figure out about child care. How do you find it? How do you start leaving this place at six at night when everybody considers that a half day of work?*" she recalls. "I looked around my department to talk to people who had kids and who figured out how to do this work-and-mom thing and I realized there was no one to talk to. There were certainly very few women with kids who were beyond the entry level and very few men whose wives had gone back to work after they had kids. I realized that it was the first time in my career I felt different from everyone else. I felt like all of a sudden I was going to try and do something different from the rest of the male culture."

May felt somewhat anxious, but more, she felt annoyed at having to figure out how to make the changes all by herself. She knew a great deal about corporate lending, but nothing at all about good child-care options and how to find them. "I had," she remembers, "no model of where to go. I never wanted to stop working; it never even occurred to me to stop working. I knew I didn't want to work the kind of hours I had been and I didn't want the unpredictability. I was very clear to my senior management, all of whom were very supportive. They were traditional guys: they were all married with kids. They all had wives who stayed home to take care of everything. I even had a boss at the time who, out of kindness asked, 'Should you be running up the stairs?' I said, 'I'm not disabled, I'm just pregnant.' He said, 'I admire that you're coming back, but I can't relate.' It just didn't seem impossible. I thought, *I can figure it out.* I was unnerved, though, by not having a support system or role models."

Eight months into her pregnancy May was offered a big promotion. She was told that she could take her maternity leave and they would hold the job for her. May considered turning it down, as she feared it would make too many demands on her, but all her male mentors told her to take it—or not be considered seriously again. May accepted the offer and went home to have her daughter.

Maternity leave lasted three months, which May found a very difficult time. "I was a typical first-time mother learning on the job, and it was a hard job. Unlike at the workplace, nobody said to me, 'You did that well today,' or 'You didn't do it well but you'll do it better tomorrow.' I figured out I had a high need for that kind of feedback." May saw she had become accustomed to the grading syndrome. "It doesn't have to be a grade but it has to be *something,* and a baby doesn't give you that. Those first six weeks were among the hardest of my life. I had a horrendous time breast-feeding and felt all this pressure. I had always done a good job at whatever I'd done and now I had to do a good job as a mother. But I was failing because I couldn't breast-feed. I felt a lot of pressure reading a Similac can, which said, 'It's the next best thing you can do for your kid.' The kid is three weeks old and already I'm already doing the *next* best thing! Yet, I was too over-achieving to realize that I needed help."

May returned to work and, then, after a year, an opportunity arose: her company (which had a hundred thousand employees internationally) decided it needed a department to "handle policy" for women who wanted to work and who wanted families as well. They offered May, now pregnant with her second child, the director's position. "Three things almost held me back," she recalls. "The first was that I was excited about being a role model proving you could do a deal-making job in four days a week. Second, I was a senior person in the department doing what I considered 'real' work as opposed to this nebulous 'work/family' work. The third thing was that I had this inner voice that said,

Second kid—she just can't cut it. She's got to go into a staff job where her life is going to be a lot easier. Although I had never consciously set out to be on the fast track, for the first time I was going to consciously step off."

The Twin Engines of Balance and Meaning

May took the job, and for the first time in years she found herself devoting her days to things other than the pursuit of traditional success. At first she felt as if she were failing—the phone wasn't ringing off the hook. She didn't have back-to-back meetings. Her calendar had open space in it. She went home in time to make dinner.

But very slowly, very gradually, May realized, "This was work I *loved.* Investment, I liked. I felt strongly about the content I was working on, the goal of having the company realize that work and family issues were terribly important—that the world wasn't all *Ozzie and Harriet.* It was critical for them to realize it was good business to help people manage their careers in all different ways. That there was no one good or bad path. It was my business-manager mind-set that said, *This is important to people, to all sorts of really good people who do good things for the company. They aren't all going to want to work sixty hours a week for the rest of their careers and they aren't all going to want to relocate when you want to relocate them.*" A deep sense of meaning infused May's work and she loved it. "From an identity point of view it was the first time in my life that I said, 'I want to do this.' Instead of somebody coming to me and saying, 'We'd like you to do this or that.' It was always me reacting to what the company was asking me to do.

176

This was the first time I said what I wanted. Actually, after all those years, it almost went back to that first career goal of being a psychotherapist." May started to define success by how much she was helping people, not by how much she was making.

Redefining Success for Herself

At the end of two years, however, the company decided to discontinue the program—for "budgetary" reasons. Devastated, May argued with her management. "This job is so important," she told them. "I can't quantify it for you, but I am sure I kept people from leaving that you didn't want to see leave. I helped people in stress, and got managers and employees talking to each other." The company responded by offering her any position she wanted. "At that point the thought of going back into investment banking just gave me apoplexy. I said, 'I think it's the wrong business decision.' But the company didn't see it that way, so it came down to a choice of doing investment work or leaving, so I left."

Having to leave infuriated May. She had worked hard for the company for twelve years and she still cared about it. Her husband still worked there, as did many of her friends. But she felt angry. "They didn't understand the business case I was making and they might as well have said, 'We don't understand her anymore. We've groomed her for twelve years and she's not the same as she was when she was a managing director doing good business like everybody else. She's tough to deal with, she wants things that we don't understand anymore. She doesn't fit into our system.'"

The senior people—all of whom were male in her office—
advised her to try to manage more territory, control a bigger
piece of the "org" chart. "But that just didn't mean a thing to me
anymore. Actually, it never really did in a sense, but I got sucked
along with it. But it was never my goal to be the first 'this' or
most important 'that.' But at this point I was doing work that I
thought was so important that I didn't care what they called me
or paid me." May tried to talk them into paying her even less and
keeping the job, but they didn't understand. "They said, 'She
spends a year negotiating a pay cut. Something's got to be wrong
with her.' "

May felt that they were saying, "It's not important to us and
therefore it shouldn't be important to you." "I was disqualified as
a member of the group, which in a sense made it easier to leave.
But the funny thing is, all of a sudden it was: what took me so
long to figure this out? I sort of clung on for too long and it
wasn't until I was on my way out that I clearly saw that I was
finally moving toward what was important to me."

When May announced she was going into business for herself, most people thought she was doing it to spend more time
with the kids. "It was nice, but that wasn't the driving force," she
said. "My entire adult life after college had been in corporations
and accepting their agendas. Now, it was up to me to do what I
thought mattered. If part of that was being available to volunteer
in my son's nursery program occasionally, so much the better.
The first day I was on my own, I had the opportunity to hear
Anna Quindlen talk about leaving *The New York Times* and it
made me feel I could do it—that this was going to be okay.

Hearing her confirmed to me that something was wrong with them, not with me."

May reclaimed what was important to her. It took her almost twenty years, but she found a way to combine her love of business, time with her family, and even her original dream of becoming a psychotherapist. But she had to trade in some things for this new life: a big title, some financial security, recognizable social worth, and the feeling of being at one with the pack. There were many moments, May admits, when she felt selfish, a bit irresponsible, and a little nuts, not to mention miserable. Even a few years later, as she tells the story, she starts to cry. "I hadn't realized that I was still hurt by all this," she apologized. "I just felt so betrayed. Not only by my company but by all my expectations. I really thought that doing the right thing was the right thing to do. But not in that world it wasn't. They just weren't about that." When I ask May if she's happier now than before, she says yes, but with a qualification. "I liked the power world. I liked having lots of influence and the possibility of changing people's lives for the better. Now I can do that, too, but on a much smaller scale. And no matter how much I love having my own business, I just don't feel like I am as much of a success as before. Of course, I don't want to be either." But the satisfaction of doing work she felt was important and the flexibility of working for herself more than made up for her departure from the male-dominated sphere of success. Acting on what was important to May freed her from living the stress-filled life. "Liberated," she exclaims. "That's how I feel. I'm free to do work I love and work I feel is important." She felt like the women Shoya Zichy describes: "The women who have done it and left it have a to-

tally different perspective. It's like you don't go to a party because you don't feel like it, not because you haven't been invited." It's too bad that for most women, misery motivates the
departure from the old paradigm. But as more women do challenge the culture's values, it will become easier and more accepted for others following behind.

Without intending to May moved from a life centered on
conventional success to one of authenticity. And a life of authenticity means a life with balance and meaning. Somewhere in the
process, what she valued inside became more important to her
than what she thought she was supposed to be or what she feared
the world would think of her. When it comes to making changes
there is no bigger challenge.

When women discover that after the work breakdown
comes the reassertion of their authentic selves, they feel a rush of
confidence and relief. There is, as author Mary Pipher says, "a
new energy that comes from making connections, from choosing
awareness over denial."[1] May's experience typifies the movement
toward the integrated life—the new model that women say they
want and don't have. She had to make choices, she had to sort out
her values. She had to turn off all the cultural expectations and
instructions that barked in her ear and directed her movements.
What was right for her male mentors wasn't right for her. And
she had to keep her sense of purpose while resisting the very
people who had provided her with opportunity. Like the course
of a river, the bends and twists of May's progress came from
erosion at the system's most pressured points. But if she hadn't
paid attention to her own desires or recognized their legitimacy,

May would have let the outside work world continue to push her into a smaller and smaller shape.

The Need for Validation

In order for a woman to find a new way of valuing herself, it makes sense that the old one must have stopped working. The desire for more balance and meaning in our lives must become strong enough, the disgust at the inequities or values of the workplace fierce enough, our sense of personal failure or exhaustion sharp enough, to overcome all the forces of cultural and internal resistance. And because the changes we make involve going from an objective standard to a subjective one, we need external support, validation, approval, and permission. We grew up being assessed, evaluated, and graded and our first impulse is to look outside ourselves for a reflection of how we're doing. "Because we don't value what doesn't make money," Shoya Zichy observes, "women need something else to give them permission to be who they really are. If you're a genius at the stock market, the world compensates you for it. But if your gift is in physical therapy, you tend not to value that as much because you aren't getting rich from it. Yet if you take the guy who is running General Motors, he could no more do that therapist's job if his life depended on it. He would not know how to teach a man to walk again or get out of his wheelchair." When we pay the therapist so poorly in comparison, we send the clear message that he or she isn't as valuable to society—that being the head of a corporation is a higher, more worthy aspiration.

Women know this isn't true. But all too often we live as though it is. Moving from a culturally approved value system to a more personal one seems almost impossible—especially when there are no real role models for us to follow. But if we don't do it, no one is going to do it for us. That old deathbed check comes in handy when we waver. Until we redefine success and value more broadly to include balance and meaning in our lives, we will stay stuck in careers that ask us to weigh one artificially divided world against another.

CHAPTER 8

Work That Works

THE WAY WE WORK IS A VESTIGE FROM another era. And we all know it. If we want work that works, however, we have to be the ones who create change. We have to stop complying with rules that ask us to tone ourselves down, we must resist our fears of who we will or won't be if we speak, and we must take responsibility for finding ways to work that incorporate what we say we value. We have played the role of the miner's canary; we have worked hard only to find there isn't sufficient oxygen to support a balanced personal and professional life as work is now structured. Transforming work is up to us.

It would be so nice and so neat if a solution existed with six simple steps that all women could follow to find work that empowered them, validated them, and fit the multiple demands and desires in their lives. But that's as much a fantasy as having it all. It isn't going to happen. The fact is that there is no single solution for women—our lives are too fluid, too varied. Some of us have no children, some of us have ten. Some of us support our families, others work for satisfaction more than a paycheck. The space families take in women's lives expands and contracts in different cycles over the years. A woman with an eighteen-month-old will approach work differently than when her child is eighteen years old. Every woman and every situation is different; we can locate ourselves at different points on a continuum at different times over the course of our lives. There can be no one model of work that works; if we tried to create one, it, too, would eventually prove too rigid to withstand the tremors of the next circumstantial earthquake.

Work will never work unless we change the way we value success and the way we judge our progress toward it. If we don't start with our values, all alteration will remain cosmetic. This is why it is so critical that women replace their emotional, psychological, and even financial dependence on our work identities with a more porous, broad, and flexible system of identifying themselves. One that prizes balance over attainment, meaning over status, inclusion over hierarchy, the product over the process. Only by shifting to these values can we create a new picture of a successful life that allows for priorities to shift over time as needs dictate. One in which work plays a key role but not an exclusive one. This is tremendously difficult, because the baby-boom women just don't have role models for this. We know success only as a version of our fathers' all-or-nothing terms. Privately, however, most of us suspect there's another way to live; that's why when someone actually steps up and out of the conventional success box, we are immediately attracted to her story.

When the actress Sherry Stringfield, who played Dr. Susan Lewis on the number-one television show *ER,* decided to trade in her big celebrity for a more normal life, she made national headlines. *"Do I want to continue going down this road?"* she asked herself. *"Or do I want to take a different road? I had a pretty good taste of what working on the show meant in my life and I just realized it's not for me."*[1] Stringfield just wanted more time for herself and her relationships; she wanted to take things at a slower pace and enjoy her life. But her simple desires shocked the nation, resulting in front-page coverage. "I recognize what I'm doing is rather unprecedented. Some people may question this from the point of view of the American work ethic. But what about the American ethic of family values? There are people who seem to think it's weird that I don't want to be famous. . . . Is it so weird for me to want more time to be free and with my family?"[2] Stringfield's choice flew in the face of our prevailing value system of money and success. And it's not that she doesn't want to work—she loves to work. She just wants to work sanely. And not to the exclusion of her life.

If, like Stringfield, we come to find our worth in many different things—not just in our work—then we are going to more fully enjoy what we do. Our sense of self, drawn from more places in our lives, will give our work less power over us. That is why the only way we are going to find work that works is by making our careers only one tile of a mosaic of life's meaning. Women really do know this. But it's so easy to get sucked into the closed circuit of success that we can easily lose our perspective. Besides, living that way makes it easier to judge how well we are doing in life—all we have to do is look up and see how we're measuring up to the culture's prefabricated images.

It's only when women find themselves, as I did, looking

down that gun barrel—"your career or your life"—that we are willing to move past those images. And immediately, we connect with our fears about being negatively judged by our own choices. And we will be. Not just by others, but by ourselves too. It seems that no matter what choice a woman makes, she is going to be criticized. I feared people would say, "She couldn't cut it," or that I had gone home, a mother by default. "I feel ashamed that I'm not doing more," one mother said to me in our children's prenursery class. "Even though I know intellectually that raising my daughters is more important to me than raising a company's net worth, I still feel like I should be doing more." Other mothers comfort themselves with studies which show that if they are happy, their children are happy. Our success culture even harshly judges women who choose the traditional man's provider role. While we approve of a man with a great career and no family, a woman with the same profile is often an object of pity—to others and herself. Even our children have absorbed this lose/lose perspective. When Stephanie left her career as a business manager for a Japanese company, her eight-year-old daughter came home from school begging her mother to go back to work. She felt embarrassed because all her friends' mothers worked. And in comparison Stephanie didn't look like she was doing enough. Another woman told the story of not receiving partnership in her law firm because after she'd been breaking her back with fifteen-hour days, the firm said they didn't want a woman partner who had so little perspective about her family. "No matter what choice we make, we're going to get nailed for it," Anna Quindlen said. "So we might as well choose what makes us happy."

Since most of us need to work, we are faced with fixing our

lives in the middle of living them. Most of us don't get to start fresh. Instead, we have to balance the scales with children, mortgages, marriages, or elderly parents hanging from them. Many women said that it seemed selfish to them to reduce their income if it meant having a four-day workweek. "What about my loved ones' quality of life?" they ask. "How can I do something that will have such a negative effect?" It's awfully easy for us to value our contributions by the amount of our paychecks rather than the amount of our time. But to get to that place of independence, of balance, we have to be willing to look squarely at the values behind *all* of our assumptions—and that means honestly looking at where sustenance leaves off and what we call "quality of life" spending begins. Somewhere we crossed an invisible line between making money so that we would be independent to a very real imprisonment. We are handcuffed to our debt and to our lifestyles and we pay dearly with our days.

The New Rules for Success

Once I faced my fears of what people would think of me and realized that those fears and my quest for cash were keeping me stuck, things began to loosen up. I began to see that there were things I could control and things I couldn't. Yes, there was sexism at work; there was prejudice, and harassment and unequal opportunity. Those remain very real issues. But I alone was responsible for clinging to the belief that if I just worked hard enough and was good enough, none of those issues would affect my career. My good-girl identity told me that I would be exempt from the barriers of sex and that if I behaved properly, I would experience the privileges my father had and work would take care of me.

The time had come to face the fact that I was seriously deluded on this issue. Even for men that promise doesn't hold true anymore. Work just wasn't going to be what I had thought it would be; and all I was doing by continuing to try to make it live up to my expectations was preserving a system that didn't have me in mind when it was created. Instead, I had to enter into a new contract, a new relationship, with my work—a relationship with some new rules. I love working too much to stay in a partnership with it that asks me to conform to values and behaviors that better suit a woman with no personal life (if there even is such a creature). This new relationship was going to mean making some trade-offs in my life; I would have to stop treasuring some used-up identities of perfectionism and being "one of the guys." Identities that had stopped being my passports to the world, and instead had become my wardens.

Looking back over the unwritten rules that I had allowed to guide my career, I saw them in a different light. I had been willing to follow them as long as I got something in return. But when that investment stopped returning, what became clear to me was that the rules had actually asked me to be less of who I was. Work couldn't work if having a good job meant burying the best parts of myself.

I started to look at some women I admired, women who didn't seem to compromise themselves. These "exceptional" women in business lived their lives by very different, new rules. I held these new ways of behaving up to several different kinds of work situations and found that they could be applied under all conditions. All the rules go against what we were taught we should do as women to fit into a man's world. So they are going to feel awkward and very unsafe at first. But if we want to come to work as ourselves, values intact, values included, we're going to have to break some old habits and take some precipitous actions.

1. Say Good-bye to the Good Girl

Probably the biggest thing keeping us trapped in unhappy situations at work is the good girl role. Because we equate speaking up with banishment (and an immediate loss of identity), we maintain silence, we fit in, we swallow the unpalatable. "There has been this awful impulse to be obedient and polite and ladylike all over again which I recognize from way back," says author Letty Cottin Pogrebin. "I see this impulse to be good girls." As long as being a good girl is high on the list of what we value about ourselves, it will be very hard to change. Because a good girl's job is to fit in, she can't—by definition—challenge anything. She will remain hermetically sealed in an environment that will never honor her.

2. Break the Vows of Silence

We can't renegotiate anything if we don't open our mouths. Starting in adolescence we learned that silencing our true selves had real payoffs. Psychologist Mary Pipher describes in great detail how crippling this silencing is for young women. It lowers self-esteem, creates a loss of authenticity. As Pipher explains, most women start to get it back in their lives at menopause, when they are allowed to "reclaim their adolescent authenticity." She points out that Margaret Mead observed this event all over the world. She even had a name for it—*pmz* or postmenopausal zest. "Because they are no longer beautiful objects occupied with caring for others, they are free once again to become the subjects of their own lives," says Pipher.[3] In the women I talked to, I actually noticed that this "zest" didn't have to wait for menopause. Just approaching or crossing the "forty"-yard line seemed to do the trick for most women. The horizon contained, their inner selves sprang loose. But why wait to speak up for ourselves? As long as we wait, we conspire with the status quo. We ensure that we remain cloaked by the conventional, and by its limitations for women. We ensure that people will be afraid to take advantage of the Family Leave Act or flex-time. We ensure that we will have two separate worlds in which we have to strive for success to feel good about ourselves. Far from being a safe haven, silence will ultimately suffocate us. There is nothing worse than being mute at the very moment when we see our dream job (the one we thought our silence would ensure) going to a more vocal and less qualified man.

3. Learn to Fail

I really believed that if I worked hard enough, I would never, ever fail. In that way I would never have to choose between things but could continue to do the impossible—routinely. Not failing was my female version of the immortality fantasy. When I came off the line, I was traveling at peak speed on the two tracks of my life, and the impact of my limitations and those of the system derailed me sufficiently that I was able to see—for the first time—that there might be another way to live. Because I had wanted to succeed so badly, it never occurred to me that the fault might lie outside myself. It never occurred to me to challenge the working world and its values, only to challenge myself. In this way when I failed—as I had to fail—I failed by myself.

Back when my value systems were installed, when I was encouraged to be whatever I wanted to be, I didn't learn the distinction between doing the best I could do and doing the best that could be done. My value, I thought, lay as much in toughing out tough situations as in the sheer number of things I could do brilliantly. There was supposed to be no end to what I could achieve. Thus, if I ever quit something, my value dropped immeasurably, immediately. I really believed that it was my duty to do it all. But when I felt backed into a corner by my own ambitions and those of the people around me, I had to reexamine that "truth."

Most of us take an enormous amount of pride in doing our work perfectly. As Leanne, a travel-guide publisher, said in utter frustration, "I bought the whole thing my parents told me. I believed being perfect was an achievable goal." But when we pay for perfection with increasingly precious hours of our days, often to have our efforts remain unrecognized, it's time to think about giving up our attachment to this rule. Behind our perfectionism usually lie two silent, conditional demands—"We'll be perfect if you never abandon us (fire us)" and "If we are perfect, you will love us forever (and recognize us with promotions and money)."

When we fail (and I'm not talking about egregious errors here but the more humdrum nature of failure—missing a deadline, telling a client that we were unrealistic, forgetting a section in the report), we think we risk abandonment and ruin. In fact, we risk some egg on our faces—or, most likely, some embarrassment in our own and others' eyes. It's astonishing the lengths to which we go to avoid being humiliated for being human. I know. I've traveled that path too many times. Many of the women I interviewed felt they had fallen into the perfect trap and didn't know how to climb out. Well, the only way is to fail regularly in small ways. Only by doing that will our definition of failure change.

"I sometimes think the only women who are truly happy are those who are comfortable with failure," Shelly Lazarus recalls one of the senior female writers in the agency as saying. "The people who are good at being working mothers are the people who are comfortable with failure because they're always failing at something—and if it does them in, then they can't continue on in these dual roles. But if they can just sort of accept it—that you are always failing somebody—you're failing your kids or your friends or yourself because you aren't there for them or you're failing your job because you aren't as focused as other people who are a hundred percent focused on it—you'll be much happier." When people are willing to trade off perfection for fullness, when women are willing to be less than perfect, then we are going to find happy working women.

4. Stop Trying to Be So "Successful"

In remarks delivered at the University of Toronto's Women's Centenary, Claudette Mackey-Lassonde, chairman and CEO of Enghouse Systems, Ltd., observed that "somehow we have forgotten to explain to young men and women that making a choice means forgoing something else. We seem to have overlooked this simple truth. Choosing to travel down one path closes off another. Some may appear to have it all—the glamorous job, the power, the status. But what they do not have is happiness, satisfaction, or purpose in what they are doing." Her message was that women pay a price for certain choices. She cited studies which show that the overwhelming majority of Canadian male executives are married, as opposed to slightly more than fifty percent of their female co-workers. She pointed out that while most Canadian male executives have children, barely half of their female counterparts do. And in sharp contrast to the low divorce rate for men, more than half the women executives' marriages had ended. "I know some of the women behind these statistics," she said. "They are the loneliest people I have ever met. I know women who didn't have children because of their careers. I know some, with children, who don't even acknowledge that they are parents. The irony is that the price of success often includes giving up family life when often the family is the reason why people work so hard in the first place."

Mackey-Lassonde's remarks were not only about paying a price, but about seeing consequences clearly. When we try to live up to the two separate pictures of success we learned as young women, we are attempting the impossible. Instead of trying over and over again to achieve these unrealistic goals, let's just stop trying and divert our energies to speaking up about what a fantasy this is. Otherwise, women will continue to blame themselves for what they fear is "falling short."

5. Take Your Personal Life to the Office with You

Another of the key rules learned on the road to prowess in our professions was to keep the private, private. Not to bring our personal and female troubles or concerns into the workplace. To handle things on our own. To compartmentalize. But as we gain self-confidence from our experience and maturity, we can start to renegotiate what is public and what is private. Idelisse Malavé observes that as we stop adhering to the external values of the success culture, we can, instead, start to create work that includes other values. "It's about making a concerted effort to reject this dynamic of public/private. I think it's about what we start to lose in girlhood. It's about trying to recapture the authority of your own experience and what you know. It's about respecting what you know. It's about going, 'This doesn't work,' and not turning around and saying, 'There's something wrong with me, I couldn't make it in the system.' Shifting to a life based on your values means accepting the authority of your own experience." This rejection of the success culture's stranglehold on what is right to bring into our work lives and what is wrong, what is successful and what is not, is the beginning of revaluing what we do with our lives.

This is already happening as more and more women infiltrate

the business culture. We have unavoidably brought our more inclusive and circular lives—lives that expand and contract as the demands of family wax and wane—to bear on the linear system. Gloria Steinem points out that "women are the last people integrated into the system. But there is no such thing as integrating women equally into the economy as it exists. But we are the most transformative and revolutionary group because we have to redefine work to include child rearing and homemaking—and insist that men do it as much as we do."

The private, hidden world of women and children has moved from the home to the office. Hire a woman and you hire her family too. The only variable is how much a woman admits that truth and acts on it. It is precisely because of women's responsibility for their parents, their children, or their friends that our increased presence in the world of work is starting to change the rules and roles for everyone.

6. Don't Do It Alone—the Importance of Community

Until enough women occupy positions of respect and power, any woman who makes any alterations in the traditional path does so in a very private and isolated way. We often depend on our bosses to dispense a "favor" or make "special allowances" for us. This necessarily separates us from our working community, either through the guilt of the favored or because we were taught not to show off in front of the less fortunate. We stay quiet about our special situations. "Take the day," I would tell an employee who really needed to be home once a week, "but for God's sake, don't tell anyone about it." The implication would be that either the privilege would be revoked or I would get in trouble with my superiors.

This demeaning system actually reinforces the power structure in its ability to grant or withhold. But it does something even more lethal—it breaks up community. And having a community is the only way women are going to feel comfortable making the changes they have to make in their lives for balance and harmony. For women to start bringing what is important to them to bear on their work worlds, they have to feel it's safe to do so, and the only way to feel safe (and not crazy to boot) is by having people around them who reinforce what they're doing.

But we were raised in a society that glorifies the individual and the individual's accomplishments. We become the self-made woman. In her 1975 book *Getting Yours: How to Make the System Work for the Working Woman,* Letty Cottin Pogrebin uses the term the *Queen Bee* (drawn from Carol Tavris's personality type) and owns up to having been one herself pre-feminism.[4] "The true Queen Bee has made it in the man's world of work while running a house and a family with her left hand. 'If I can do it without a whole movement to help me,' runs her attitude, 'so can all those other women.' " A Queen Bee relishes "the fact that she is 'special,' that she has unique qualifications that allow her to get high-ranking positions normally denied to women." If a woman is a Queen Bee, she is immediately separated from other women and thus there's no hope of a group coming together in the name of change. It's tragic how little has changed in twenty years.

All this serves to underscore how much of ourselves we have

traded for our success. We are using all our good energy to prop up and perpetuate a system that rewards us for chopping out or marginalizing the private part of our lives. As we ascend the ladder in our professions, we get farther away from values that we admit in the privacy of interviews and questionnaires are the most important things to us. Yet we don't talk about it with other women, except to point out what inflexible jerks our managers are. By not talking with other women we perpetuate the very thing that keeps work from working for women. We cement the exclusion of our values from our definition of success.

Women need to look to either side of themselves, however, and see that they already have plenty of company in rejecting the rigidity and narrowness of the success culture. Women like May and Ellie and Jane. But, as Shoya Zichy points out, women need to have validation. Because the entire culture reinforces the male values, a woman trying to change her values in a vacuum is doomed. "Sure you have to make some shifts inside, but you do it with people," urges Idelisse Malavé. "It doesn't have to be so separate. If we could make some effort to stop these false separations—public/private, mind/body, community/individual—if women could start understanding at a deeper level the meaning of 'the personal is political,' that's what takes it to another place. As long as women struggle to come up a new model individually, it won't work," she cautions. "You don't transform a society, a culture, a community, through individual actions. This is a shared problem, but what we insist upon doing is trying to come up with individual solutions to a collective problem. It's not very strategic. To sit there and go 'Okay, everyone, there's oppression and discrimination against women. And me? I'm going to work very hard, and if I work three times harder than men and I'm really smart, I can overcome this.' "

Acting collectively makes things better for everyone. In the working paper *Re-Linking Work and Family,* Lotte Bailyn of the Alfred P. Sloan School of Management at MIT and her associates proved that "without a collective understanding that personal issues affect all employees . . . it will not be possible systematically to relate them to the work systems and practices in the work environment."[5] (Bailyn defines *family* as anything to do with a personal life.) In fact, they found that "framing work-family issues as individual concerns requiring individual accommodations actually had several unintended negative consequences not only for the workers' personal lives and the goal of a gender-equitable workplace but also for business goals themselves." The group found that the benefits of group discussion, if not community action, relieved people of their perception that their individual needs were the problem.

But many women are still uncomfortable with the thought of acting together. We have depended for years on our individual accomplishments. We have been rewarded for them, praised for them, promoted for them. Many of us remember the disparaging remarks made about women who tried collective actions. Pogrebin feels the media is to blame in killing collectivity because any time a woman says she's a feminist, the image that comes to mind is that of a humorless spoilsport. Indeed, Pogrebin says her greatest regret is that she sees little willingness on the part of women to create a national grassroots movement that will transform our lives to include the values we say are most important to us. "I see women who get angry when things happen to them and they are alone with their anger and frustration and they swallow it and think this is just something they have to put up with. It doesn't occur to them to check the woman at the next desk, in the next office, or down the hall to see if two or three or eight of them have the same complaint." Women don't want to risk censure, they don't want to risk the privileges they've worked hard to get. "Women don't want to be seen as whistle-blowers because they see what happens to whistle-blowers. Without collective action," Pogrebin concludes, "you just become a troublemaker."

My husband and I once had a nasty spat over what he felt was an absurd need to talk through my life and my options with my friends. But the fact is, without their support I wouldn't have had the clarity or courage to transform the shape of my life and reorder and revalue my priorities along the lines that best suited me. Since I was probably not going to get much encouragement from my office, I needed reinforcement from those who love me. There were other women with whom I shared all the stages—the slow descent into lethargy, the feeling of being overwhelmed, and the seemingly bizarre decision to quit our jobs. We had each other as a support as we tested options, tried opinions, sought answers outside the traditional world of work.

We need community to change cultural values. "A value isn't a value unless it is organized and acted upon," Marie Wilson wisely points out. "That's what the church is, an organizer of values." If women talk to each other, then what looks like individual choices actually becomes a value system. The changes we make in our lives become part of something greater than the sum of the parts. Only in this way can we transform and enlarge our definition of success.

7. Live by What You Treasure

Nothing is going to change if we don't live by what we value, if we don't say out loud, "I can't do a strategic planning meeting on Saturday, it's my kid's soccer game." Or "I have class on Tuesday nights, so I have to leave at five-thirty." While this seems much easier to do if you have a child (I never hesitated to inform whoever was unfortunate enough to call me at 5:42 P.M. that they had exactly three minutes before I had to walk out the door), it's an option available to everyone. But to take advantage of it we have to get over the thrall of the macho marathon work schedule. Does this mean someone who is around at seven o'clock in the evening might get the promotion you had worked for so hard? Possibly. But it also means that every time we exercise the option to draw a boundary between work and the rest of life and make our lives priorities, we win back a little more control. As Marian Woodruff, a Denver accountant, said, "I feel like I've had two dogs in my life—a really sweet, patient, loving one and a fierce, rough, growling one. For years I fed the mean dog in order to keep it calm, in order that it wouldn't hurt me. But what I realized after many years was that the nice dog was getting weaker and weaker because he wasn't being nourished. I'd been feeding the wrong dog."

Shelly Lazarus keeps her priorities very clear: she doesn't go out on Saturday evenings and spends the weekends with her family—no matter what. "I've lost some friends because of it, I'm sure," she says. "But I have to be very clear about what's most important to me." Lazarus loves her work and always has; she lives by her values. "A lot of women come and talk to me about balance," she comments. "I always say that the first thing you need to do is know what your priorities are and then you have to have the courage to make sure that other people understand them so that you can behave in ways that are consistent with your priorities. If you're afraid to say to your boss, 'I'm not going to be here because I have to be at the school play,' you're going to have problems."

Lazarus recalls a speech she gave when she was named Advertising Woman of the Year. "I told the story about having been assigned to the largest account at the agency. I'm there at the first meeting with the man who was in charge of all marketing for the company and he said, 'It's great that you are joining us now because three weeks from now we're going to have an all-day off-site meeting where the twenty people who care most about this business are going to sit around the table and write the five-year strategic plan.' And I said, 'That's very nice, but I can't get there until one o'clock.' He asked why and I told him that it was my son's field day. The man said, 'You're kidding, right?' I told him that I wasn't. I said, 'I'm not kidding at all, it's my son's field day and the truth is that three weeks after the meeting, you won't even remember who was in the room from nine to one and if I don't go to my son's field day, he will never forget.' " At that point in the speech Lazarus realized that several women in the audience had started to cry. "Do you know why they were upset?" she asked me. "They didn't go to field day. But still, people are too afraid to think that way. It takes a lot of courage to go up to that client and say you aren't coming until one o'clock," she mused. "I think I did those women a disservice because I made them more conflicted. I know that some of them think, *Shelly*

Lazarus, she can pull it off, because of who she is, but I haven't won the right yet. But I was always that way. And that's why I think I've always loved working."

When we endow our work with the power either to validate us or deny us opportunity, we give up the chance to become self-confident, and truly independent. Until we prioritize our lives according to what is important to us individually, we will remain in need of the external reinforcement we get from our jobs. We are all too aware of what we sacrifice for work, but if we don't put those things on the agenda, work will always come first. If Shelly Lazarus is right, we can have it both ways. As long as we live first by what we treasure, and let the rest fall into place.

8. There Is No Such Thing as "Women's Work"

In order to create real change we will have to enlarge our definitions of success to include what society has devalued as "women's work." If we give equal value to the business of taking care of community and others, running homes, maintaining relationships, and other "unwaged" or relatively poorly paid pursuits, we immediately create more "successful" choices that are of benefit to both women and men. When men started going into the nursing field in the 1970s, for example, the pay rose steadily and the stigma a man might have felt being in a "woman's" job began to recede. Thus, opportunities for men increased and women's compensation grew. We have no hope of creating an externally balanced work world for women if we don't assign an equal internal value to the unpaid work of contributing to our communities and our homes. We say we prize caring and meaning more than anything else; if we don't act on those things, then they will continue to be shoved to the corners of our workdays.

9. Work Outside the Box

For better or for worse—and it can be argued both ways—most women start their careers in the nine-to-five structured corporate world. We accept the two weeks of vacation a year, the annual raises, the corporate ladder, the success food chain, because that's the form we're used to. And that's also most of what is offered to the young graduate. But that model is only as holy as we make it. If we are willing to risk conventional success—status, title, money, power—we might find that there are others who have success on their own terms in their own form.

Stopping Out

Taking a break of longer than a month is an option only with careful financial planning. The attendant risks are reentry, reentry, and reentry. The most common form of stopping out is taking time (the most common is eighteen months) to be with a child. Some mothers work a day a week, other women, like a group of attorneys in Washington, D.C., start organizations like Lawyers at Home that help women keep connected, involved, and mutually supported. These women recognize that many are sacrificing partnership opportunities, but another way to look at what they are doing is to see it as a challenge to the single direction, nonstop career path. Stopping out reflects the more circular life of women—it is realistic about the fact that there are extra stresses for women with families at different times in their lives.

The other women who stop out are like Ellie; burnt out and whipped from years of workaholism. Stopping out requires some careful planning, and it's not just financial. Janet Andre recommends that a woman keep an anchor in her old world—whether with a professional association, community group, or a network—more for psychological than professional reasons. "Without an anchor to help with transition many women just panic after a year or so and run back to their old world," she observes. Because our lives have been defined for so long by what we do, many women who try this option feel "invisible" when they stop working and their self-esteem drops precipitously. Rather than wait out the uncomfortable period until we start defining ourselves by different terms, it's understandable that we begin to look fondly on our old identities and sometimes return to the familiarity of even an unfulfilling work life—associating with the devil we know often feels better than the false feeling that we are suddenly nobodies who belong nowhere.

The benefits of stopping out, however, can be enormous. Rachel felt completely burnt out after eight years as a lawyer for a huge corporate law firm. "I had worked on one case, an antitrust case, for seven of the eight years I was at the firm. None of the men who were married when the case started were married when the case ended. Three of the four women assigned to the case left. I had to get as far away as I could. The firm gave me a year off—I think they were freaked out that so many women were leaving. So I went to teach English in China for a year, which turned into two." Upon returning to the States she was reluctant to resume her old schedule and lifestyle, but she had to earn some money and she felt some loyalty to the firm for having told her she could have her job back. What she found was that her newly acquired Mandarin made her very appealing to the company, which represented a large corporation trying to do business in China. Because she had been out of the cultural orbit of her office for a couple of years, she wasn't as invested in making partner or being a top woman at the firm anymore. Instead, she was able to work a reduced schedule exclusively for the client interested in Asia. The work went so well that when Rachel decided she wanted a bigger challenge, she went in-house for the corporation and now she divides her time between Los Angeles and Hong Kong. "If I hadn't taken the time off and realized that I could live without my job, I would never have ended up where I am. I recommend it highly," she said with a smile.

Alternative Work Arrangements

Stopping out is great, but most women can't swing it financially. More practical for many women is setting up an alternative work arrangement. That can mean anything from flex time to reduced hours to telecommuting or job sharing. Most companies have policies on their books to accommodate any one of these options. The reason they don't get used, however, is people are too frightened that they will not be offered interesting work or new opportunities because they aren't putting their work first. Their fears are well founded. In Marcia Brumit Kropf's research for Catalyst, she has found that the biggest stumbling block in making alternative work arrangements a viable option for women lies in the value system of the success culture. "A shift in values has to precede any structural change," she points out. "Otherwise you come right up against the prevailing values. We have to reeducate the workforce about what's important. I can think of many companies that have wonderful policies—you read their employee handbooks and think, *How wonderful!* But few people will take advantage of those programs because they feel the impact on their professional lives will be too negative." Kropf points out that when a woman does take advantage of a flexible arrangement, she often finds herself the focus of a department's anger. Her co-workers resent having to pick up for someone who isn't there. The solution to that problem lies in shifting how we are judged for our work. We need to focus on the product that is produced, not the process that produces it. The team model experiment Xerox tried resulted in record-breaking reduction in the amount of time it took to bring a new product to market. Texas Instruments, too, has used alternative structures to stunning success. "Flexible work arrangements are a 'letting go' kind of model," Kropf points out. "It's saying, 'Here's our vision; at the end of the process we want to achieve the following goal.' That way you aren't judged if you are there from Monday to Friday or from seven to seven. You are judged by what you produce." That kind of out-of-the-box thinking challenges the traditional model in the workplace, and challenges the whole command-and-control nature of today's work structure. It allows women more flexibility in when and where they work. Flexibility that women say would make almost all the difference in whether they stayed in a company or not.

Women won't take advantage of these alternative arrangements if they continue to adhere to the old rules. We have to ask ourselves what is more important—looking good in the eyes of our corporations, or working in ways that cut down the stress of having home and personal lives. We know the answer, we just need to have the courage of our conviction.

Work for Yourself

Of course, there are many companies that absolutely don't allow job sharing or flex time. A very real option for us, then, is to work for ourselves. One out of every four people in the United States who works for someone else now works for a woman who owns and manages her business[6] according to Dr. Sharon G. Hadary, executive director for the National Foundation for Women Business Owners. She reports that their research shows that one of the reasons women start their own businesses is because they aren't comfortable with the corporate environment. While other women cite the glass ceiling as the reason they went into business for themselves, and others the need for flexibility, Hadary sees another compelling motivator—control over their lives. Hadary observes, "When we ask these women what the greatest reward of working for themselves is, they talk about having control over their own destinies." Considering most women work in order to be independent, having your own business takes that need a step further. Steinem concurs, "The more pathbreaking, crucial alternative is women who are either starting their own businesses, freelance in some way, or who have cooperatively owned businesses—whatever form it takes. These women are outside the going structures. If we're ever going to have a really powerful movement, some of us have to have jobs we can't be fired from. It's absolutely crucial."

Women who have their own businesses can be the models of how business can be both humane and efficient. Even more, however, women who have their own businesses can decide for themselves what to spend their energies on and how to define success. Hadary has seen that women who own their companies do have different values and that values themselves are more important to women business owners than to men. "I think many women who start their own businesses are redefining success. A lot of people point to the fact that while we are seeing tremendous growth in the numbers and size of women–owned businesses, they don't seem to grow as fast as companies owned by men. We don't seem to see as many 'gazelles.' When I talk to women, though, there is a real concern for *responsible* growth. 'What really sets us apart,' they say, 'what gives us our competitive edge, is our quality and our personal involvement with the clients.' These women want to make sure they grow in a way that doesn't harm relationships." As Hadary points out, it's not that these women don't want their businesses to grow, they just don't value growth as an end in itself. They measure success more in what kind of business they run, whether they are doing something meaningful.

Research shows that women who start their own businesses are coming from everywhere: corporate downsizing, women who look around at the upper levels of management and don't see anyone who looks like them. They are also leaving corporations because sometimes they feel they can do it better or differently.

They are coming from home. And a significant number of them are "mature" women, fifty years old and up. We don't have to wait until we are forced out to start our own businesses. By working for ourselves we can put our values into action; we can broaden the definition of work, enrich what we call success, and become models for the next generation.

Transformation

All these alternatives point a path to the future. "How work gets changed is more important than just for women," emphasizes Marie Wilson. "It's whether or not we're going to have a way to have work, period. We're experiencing a huge shift right now. There are lots of pieces working together right now: the fact is, there will never be enough jobs again, ever. There will have to be a sharing of work if we ever want people to have enough work. Therefore, there has to be something outside of work that becomes a valued part of who you are—not just 'Hello, what do you do?' And to make this change we will really have to revalue and restructure values for our whole society." Wilson feels the constellation of job insecurity, the changing role of men, and the numbers of women in the workforce is coming together in a way that will start to shift our culture's value paradigm.

It seems so obvious, so simple, so sensible: So, why hasn't it been done? The answer, quite simply, is that never before has a group of women tried to have success on the scale we have tried to have success. The only model we had was one that fit men. And it took us some time before we accomplished enough to discover that the model didn't fit us. We entered a work culture whose attractive benefits we desired and we deserved. But with those privileges came a value system that we accommodated and then assimilated. Men have had no culturally accepted alternative to living the linear lives devoted to the pursuit of "more," so their only choice has been to resist the threat of change.

But now that enough women have experienced the very real limitations of the success system, they have begun to see that even the promise of equality itself wasn't real—and maybe not worth giving up their lives to have. We have started to see that women are still kept away from the positions of real power. A 1996 *Working Woman* magazine survey of the top jobs for women was embarrassing—their net worth, spheres of influence, though exponentially greater than thirty years ago, don't begin to compare to men's. Because changing women's roles means changing men's, the entire culture resists it. "It has ever been thus, that when the less powerful group imitates the powerful, it's the sincerest form of flattery," Steinem observes. "But when the powerful start imitating the powerless, it's called subversion, revolution, which is why it's as crucial for men to become more like women as it is for women to become more like men. That is, full human beings." And since revolution means unseating those with power, keeping the structures and their values intact becomes an act of pure survival.

There are now enough women in the workforce that none needs to feel she is fighting an isolated battle to break down the forms of work in order to better do the content. But two things will have to change for this transformation to continue and to be maintained: women will have to break the stranglehold of the culture's success values—which they can do only with support from other women—and men will have to see there is something in this transformation for them.

"From a public-opinion-poll point of view, the majority of the country now absolutely believes that women can do what men can do, but the next step is to believe that men can do what women can do," says Steinem. "That is the next psychic leap forward that we need." By equally valuing the two worlds, women and men can combine parts of each without risking their sense of self-esteem and value, without risking the approval and respect of their peers and society. By giving equal value to the two worlds, we could identify ourselves based on doing what we hold important, and not what society thinks we should treasure.

The forces of gender and custom have artificially divided us from ourselves and from each other. Women have been told we aren't real women if we don't have children. Or we aren't good mothers if we go to work. Or we aren't successful women if we don't have big or important jobs. The culture has also told men who elect to stay home with children that they aren't real men. We have allowed and have been rewarded for letting the outer hand dominate the inner hand. While economic opportunity in the Western world seemed endless, we could afford this synthetic fantasy. But the twin forces of economic uncertainty and sufficient numbers of women who have achieved conventional success combine to make the time ripe for transformation.

Women are on the front lines of this transformation because we are the miner's canaries—we are trying to do what hasn't been done before in history. And many of the most talented and accomplished among us are bowing out from lack of nourishment and exhaustion. We cannot do it by ourselves. Alone, we can make amendments and improvements, but we are still basically offered an alternative of take it or leave it.

"The workplace is not going to change until a critical mass of men also demand it," says Gloria Steinem. "But they will see that there are rewards. They get to know their children. They won't end up thirty years from now with an engraved watch and nothing else." Men see this. But we have a culture geared to the continuation of the provider role. It's only as these men's wives, sisters, girlfriends, and female co-workers challenge the structures and values of the success culture that men are going to feel they have permission to make some changes as well.

If women don't voice their problems and give men a chance to identify with them, then nothing will change. If women don't draw some lines in the sand and stop trying to be all things to all people, nothing will change. Why should it? What most men have received as a result of the increased presence of women at work is a second income and a higher lifestyle. Why would anyone want to give that up? Women haven't asked them to and they haven't offered. As Steinem described it, "First the male dominant culture that we all absorb in our pores says, 'No, you cannot be an editor, a mechanic, a line repair person. You're a woman, you can't do that.' Then, we do it anyway. Next the culture says, 'All right, but you have do to everything you did before, because we don't want to be disturbed here. You can be an editor, a lines person, or mechanic, but only if you continue to do everything you did before—cook all the meals, take care of men, have children and take care of them, dress for success, and be multiorgasmic till dawn.' As long as women are trying to do two jobs, men don't have to change."

But now that this baby-boom generation of women has started to question, if not challenge, the values of the success culture, a renegotiation can begin. We can find work that works if we break some of the old rules, and we can create cultural change if we encourage the men around us to follow suit. There's plenty of benefit for men in changing our narrow definition of success, in altering the way we work, but we have to lead the way. The first stage of women's entry into the male success sphere didn't require men to change, just slide down the bench a bit and make some room. The next stage, the transitional stage, has to engage the men and affect their roles and responsibilities profoundly.

CHAPTER 9

Men, Work, and Identity

MY HUSBAND MAKES A GOOD LIVING. IT'S a great statement. It simultaneously locates his exact worth in the world and represents the complete appeasement of my father's concerns for his daughter. Some burdens still pass from man to man. While I was learning that I could do the same job as any guy for the same pay, I also inhaled the fragrance of security (and potential luxury) promised by marrying a man with a good job. These two understandings bestowed on me a sense of freedom, of choice. Not that I wanted to depend on a man. I spent two decades fending for myself, enjoying the profound benefits of being a woman of independence. But I'd be less than honest if I didn't say that somewhere deep in the back of my brain, nestled in the darkest folds, lay the comforting notion that somehow, some way, I would be taken care of one day.

Until my husband became the sole source of consistent income in our family, though, I had never really considered what that equation "good provider equals security" meant from anyone else's point of view, notably my husband's. Because I had been making a good salary, he hadn't had to face his unaired assumptions about it either. But the day I woke up jobless and depressed with no vision of what I planned to do in the future, he—who so actively supported my leaving—went to work in a bit of a blue funk. Which, over time, blackened to an inky cloud.

History, cultural expectations, and experience accounted for the change in his weather: my husband had been here before. Like some other men at the front of the baby-boom curve, he had lived under two different sets of rules in two different incarnations, all before he'd even officially hit midlife. In his first marriage he played the role of the traditional male provider. His wife stayed home and raised their children. He never thought twice about being the one who went off to the office every day. His life was not so different from his father's and neither were his expectations, obligations, or responsibilities. He lived surrounded by a company of men who rode the same trains, coached the same soccer games, turned in the same expense reports. They were doing what they were raised to do. They were doing what was right and worthy.

"What are you so worried about?" he'd ask me in frustration when I protested that he just didn't understand, I *had* to work for my own self-esteem, for my sense of independence. "I make enough money for you to stay home if you want." At the time he was not thinking about the psychological importance work held for me. But, to be fair, I underappreciated how extremely hard he had worked over many years to be able to say that sentence with all the confidence he could. My husband loves me and when I was miserable, he wanted to give me the gift of the freedom to work out the confusion in my life without having to ride the subway every day.

But when I took him up on his offer, that small, dark cloud collected on his emotional horizon. Now it really *was* up to him. Now he couldn't entertain fantasies of joining the senior pro golf tour or becoming a therapist or a stockbroker or Mr. Mom. Although he had gladly taken the complete financial weight of our lives onto his shoulders, something deep within him simultaneously bridled at the extinction of even the possibility of freedom. A grimness set in, his mood heavy with the knowledge his options had just shrunk to almost zero.

Reading this, I think my husband will protest that he had no reservations whatsoever about his offer—which will be the truth. But that doesn't mean that underneath everything there wasn't also a quiet, slow deflation as the second income slowed to a trickle and then dried up completely. An income that had represented a potential safety valve and cushion. Even though he was doing what was expected—more, he was doing what he wanted—it just wasn't fair, on some level, that I got to quit and he didn't.

Some days I would joke around and say that when I was rich, he could stop work and play golf every day. "I can't wait!" he'd respond, and go off to work. But even though most men will say something like that, it would be very hard for them to actually do it. So much of who they are depends on what they do—or don't do. Most of my husband's human contact takes place in his office—it's his main community. He's worked with the men and women there for more than twenty years—they are a big part of his life. Besides that, my husband's position confers on him an identity and a sense of worth. He's proud of the fact that he can afford to support the people he loves; it makes him feel that his days have meaning and purpose. When his work is going well, it gives him great personal satisfaction. It confirms to him that he has a place in this world, a job to do. He's busier than he wants to be, travels much more than he likes, but in spite of the hassles his work fires him up in a place that very few other things in life can reach. For him—and for many of his friends—to assume any role other than that of the main provider means an enormous rear-rangement of values and pride and identity has to take place. For these men, work gives more than self-definition and fulfillment; it brings (as women well know) independence and a measure of control over life. It's a right women fought hard to get. And I've yet to meet a man who wanted to part with any control whatso-ever as far as his life and career were concerned.

My husband is an extremely smart man. He is quite aware that there are many alternatives to the way he works. He knows that there are ways to cut his income that would result in more time at home, more time with me, with our child. He appreciates that I could be the one to go to work every day and that he could raise our son. He understands that there is still very little societal support for any of those alternatives. For a man like my husband, the first one in his family to go to college, the first one to break into the executive ranks, those choices represent a diminishment of the possible. More than that, they represent a step off the path of the American Dream. Becoming a success, making the most of the hard-won opportunities in his life, is more than a badge of honor, it's something that gives esteem, meaning, shape, and purpose to his life. In the face of that kind of power it's pretty easy to let these alternatives remain simply ideas.

Little boys still get the message by our example that their career paths and their lifelines lie locked together. Even though women now comprise half the workforce, rather than broaden the message to include other values, or rearrange the top priority we assign to the gathering of money, power, and success, we have simply extended the same set of values to little girls. If we, the adults, haven't broadened our definition of a successful life to include with equal worth the values of caring for community, connection, and service; if we continue to value the ten hours we work to buy a car with a CD stereo less than the equipment they purchase; what choice do we really give anyone who moves away from the success we worship as a society?

When my father came home to this country after fighting in World War II, he went to law school on the GI Bill. He knew opportunities his parents never had known. He had known poverty and promise. He delighted in giving me an easier life than he'd had. My father believed that social and economic mobility knew only one true direction—up. It was his duty to make sure his family benefited—not for power's naked sake but for the sustenance and pleasure and growth of those he loved. But long after I have been self-supporting, my father still works as though my life depended on it. For the men of my father's generation, being a man and being a provider were almost synonymous. For him, who he is and what he does are fused so completely that I have often thought that the moment he stops working he will stop breathing. It wouldn't surprise me. I've seen it before.

219

A Business Built for Providers and Heroes

Author Warren Farrell cited a study that demonstrated that the image and equation of masculinity as breadwinner in this country was so powerful that it would actually be easier for a man to have his sex changed than to undo the social and cultural conditioning about what it meant to be a man in our society.[1] Even though what we call a traditional family—with the homemaker mom and sole-provider dad—accounts for less than three percent of American families today,[2] this tenacious image is the one centrally installed in most baby boomers' mental wiring. According to this picture, men get their identities and their worth mostly from the work they do. Society rewards men with its approval according to how much influence a man wields, how important a man's work is to the community, or how much money he produces.

In May of 1996, when Admiral Jeremy Boorda committed suicide, I couldn't help but think that he represented a tragic, if extreme, example of how dangerous the work-equals-life equation had become. A proud man, an accomplished man, Boorda was a true American success story. He rose through the ranks to the top of the Navy by the sweat of his own efforts, the first enlisted man in its history to do so. When it was charged that he might not have been entitled to wear certain of the medals he sported, rather than blacken the office to which he had devoted forty years of his life, he killed himself. When something threatened to go hideously wrong with his job, there was no other side of him that he could rely on to sustain him as a human being. "He so identified with the uniform he wore . . . that in the end, he was apparently unable to separate his real self from his naval persona," *Newsweek* magazine concluded.[3] For Boorda the stain of dishonor at work was enough to render his whole life a tragic failure.

Boorda is of the generation that still presides over most of business. His values—while exaggerated—aren't so different from the values of the men who exclusively inhabit the top seats at *all* of the *Fortune* 500 companies and a huge majority of the positions in the upper echelons. While we justly focus on the implications of that skewed amount of power on women's lives, for the first time in history research is showing that younger men (beginning with the baby boomers) are also being negatively affected by outdated work and family values. For that generation, what a man did for a living wasn't merely about putting food on the table. What and how much he provided determined the importance, value, and meaning of his life and of his children's.

This is the way that work—and by extension, manliness—became endowed with a kind of sacredness and power way beyond its actual activities. The moment that survival was no longer the exclusive reason men left home every day, work and masculinity became synonymous. If work failed, the man failed. That is what makes Boorda's death such a modern morality tale. The tragedy lies not in his dishonor but in the fact that he didn't *have* to die for what he did or didn't do (some contend he had actually earned the right to wear the medals). He didn't die for his country, he didn't die for his family, he died for his office. Although Boorda died by his own hand, is he so very different from the legions of men who kill their days or the quality of their lives in return for more money, more power or prestige? What about the thousands of men who sit grim faced in traffic jams, commuter trains, or the subways every day on their way to the offices to fulfill their role as the male provider? Or the men who travel for work and spend many weeks, if not months, away from their families and friends?

Warren Farrell says, "Men are taught to be human doings; women are taught to be human beings." He feels the paradox of masculinity is that "a man becomes 'someone' by forfeiting himself to a corporation, the armed services, or other organizations." He points out that the word *hero* derives from the Greek *ser-ow,* servant or slave. In Farrell's view, "Work has never worked for men as human beings. The very purpose of work, historically, has been survival; men sacrificed themselves and their time to feed their families. In exchange, they received respect, approval, love, and immortality in the memories of others." Farrell feels men's problem is that they have learned to define power as "feeling obligated to earn money." Thus, in his view, the more a man gives up his life to work, the more "heroic" he becomes and the more society esteems him. Today's work environment continues to create and perpetuate that kind of "heroism," and a working man is still judged—and loved—for what he produces for others. This stereotype hasn't changed much since the 1950s. But for today's baby-boom generation, it no longer is a comfortable fit.

"The corporate world, stuck in the mentality of the 1950s, too often still operates on the notion that the American worker is a male with a wife at home to tend to all the family issues,"[4] observes psychologist Rosalind C. Barnett, author of a major NIH-backed study of men, women, and work. Studies like hers and others show that neither men nor women believe anymore in that model of work where work is most holy. Yet, as Barnett observes, it's "hard to rip out of our heads the images that we believe to be eternal truth—which are, in fact, merely the residue of an atypical time."[5]

Authors Barnett and Rivers report their research categorically showed that "it is simply not true that a job is more important to a man than his family."[6] But they emphasize how unaware business today seems to be of this fact. While seminars are offered on ways to reduce stress, stop smoking, or meditate, there is virtual silence on the topic of balancing work and family—the domain, these companies feel, of women. "Until men realize that family issues are not the sole domain of women, nothing is going to change," state the authors. They go on to say that until corporations rearrange their priorities and men realize that the unwritten rules are killing their chances at any semblance of balance, "the emotional health of American men will remain in jeopardy."[7]

Moreover, the landmark study found that the "traditional" division between men and women—that men work and do and women care and feel—simply no longer exists. Quite emphatically, the research showed that a man's home life, a man's marriage, and a man's children are as important to his sense of happiness and his identity as they are to a woman's.[8] The study echoed what other current research shows, that "more men are willing to trade raises and promotions to spend time with their families."[9] These are the private and true beliefs of men today. But they run headlong into the definition of being a good man (a good provider) that these men received growing up. That definition just might have made sense forty years ago when in exchange for hard work a man could expect to be taken care of by his company for life. But in the light of the new economic realities of downsizing and the extinction of corporate loyalty, cleaving to this definition is punitive. The clash of the way men really identify themselves today and the old messages that run around in their heads is leaving them with the feeling they are caught in pincers, squeezed between who they are supposed to be and who they want to be, how they are supposed to work and how they want to live. Today, it is just plain dangerous for a man's sense of well-being to give his work the kind of power to determine his self-worth and identity.

My husband found this out the hard way. In the middle of my writing this book, he discovered that his position was being rearranged off the organization chart. With a tap of the delete key much of who he was and much of what he cared for was wiped away. Since he knew about the change before most others in his company, he had to pretend to be who he had been for quite a while. Standing by him at a corporate function one night, I could see the way people treated him with respect and deference. He had earned both. A man came up to me and told me how much people thought of my husband. I wondered if he would say such nice things if my husband were no longer the number-two man in his company. I wondered if my husband wondered the same thing. I knew in that moment that it was going to take a while for him to sort out the man and the work. It had been a long time since he'd had to.

Separating the Role and the Man

Because the messages about work and masculinity are so knotted up and tangled together, any examination of the subject makes most men touchy at best. They may want to leave work, but they don't feel they can without giving up a good deal of what they were taught it means to be a man. When author Wendy Kaminer left the practice of law to become a writer, she found herself the object of male envy. "I can't tell you the number of male lawyers who used to come up to me," she recalls. "They'd say, 'I'm so jealous; I've always wanted to do that!' and I'd say, 'It's easy. Just quit your job and go live in a garret.' They had all these fantasies about it. Really, they were as free to do it as I was. Except they weren't." The images about what it meant to be a successful man depended too heavily for these men on having a successful work life. And a successful work life was not defined by an insecure income. Consequently, men are boxed in, left with a Hobson's choice—work hard and be seen as a success or be less than a real man.

Unlike men, women have a socially (if not personally) acceptable alternative—go home and be a wife and mother. When I left my job, I had an immediate identity—inaccurate and incomplete as it was—as a mother. The fact that I became a writer and continued to work full-time got lost under the more socially obvious other role. Had my husband been the one to quit, he would have had a very different experience—he would be an unemployed ex-something. He would still be defined by what he once did.

This link between identity and work is beginning to break

225

down, however, as the baby-boom generation experiences an insecurity in work that their fathers never did. A January 1997 *New York Times* poll reported that 80 percent of men and women interviewed said they knew someone who had—or they had themselves—lost a job in the last two years. The sacrifice involved in a hero's life makes increasingly less sense when it goes unrecognized or discounted. If a man works hard (or sees his friends doing so) and loses his job anyway, the incentive for propping up the model that worked a generation ago drops to nearly nothing. Still, getting past the silent and lethal corollary to the provider equation—the one that says that failure to succeed proves that the man himself is the failure—means enormous rewiring for men. For many it's still better to die trying. And if the insurance industry's figures are correct, that is precisely what men are doing—an average of four years earlier than women.

But men do know something is wrong. Ask a man with a young daughter if he wants her to be able to do what he does for a living. "Of course," he will say. Then ask him if he wants her to work the *way* he works. It won't take him very long to say, "No way." For an increasing number of men work is beginning to be something that is simply not worth dying for.

One of the amazing statistics affecting men today is that 48 percent of women in married couples provide half or more of the family income. And if a woman is separated, divorced, widowed, or heads a single-parent household, the percentage is even higher—64 percent.[10] More and more, women are the benefit providers. This profound change causes some necessary confusion as the roles come loose from their economic anchors. When economic factors are no longer driving the roles each person plays in a relationship, we begin to see how stubborn the old messages are. We have internalized them and we find them echoed to us from the structures and attitudes in our employment and our communities. In actual practice, however, the exclusivity of the bread-winner-as-man model is finished forever.

Indeed, when a man no longer *has* to be the provider, who is he and why does he work? Michael Lancaster, a fifty-year-old corporate strategist for an international technology company, has spent a good deal of time, recently, asking himself those questions. After almost thirty years in his company he was tired of all the travel and the pressure in his office, but he had two years left before the generous stock benefits offered to him were fully vested. Mike had enough money to be comfortable, though, and his wife, Linda, made a very good living as a very successful software designer. They had been talking about leaving the New York area for a different life and had just decided on a two-year plan to do so when they found out that Mike's position was being eliminated because of a reengineering. He wasn't being asked to leave—in fact the president of the company went out of his way to tell Mike how valuable he was to them—but he was being offered positions of much less responsibility and importance.

Rather than see this event as an opportunity to cut down on what had been bothering him about his job, Mike was devastated. "I feel a horrible loss of domain," he said. "And I hate the fact that people are talking behind my back." Because some of Mike's peers were benefiting from the change, they had known that his job was being eliminated well before Mike did. "I feel betrayed and deceived. I had been a partner with these guys for years. It's kind of humiliating."

Mike's wife, Linda, shakes her head as she muses, "You know, it's not just Mike who is affected by this. Our whole family is shaken up. It's not the money either. I make enough for us to live on and besides, the company I work for is about to be bought and I have lots of stock because I was here in the beginning. It's more about Mike's ego and sense of importance. Our eleven-year-old son said to me the other day, 'I hope Dad doesn't do something stupid.' Even he relied on Mike's position—he bragged about him to his friends. But Mike is so hurt, we can all feel it. I don't need him to have this big job to love him. But I do need him to like himself. And I think he's going to be absolutely lost without a big job. It made him feel important. Respected. He took so much pride in building the company and helping people. I don't know what he's going to do to replace that; so much of what he thinks is best about him comes from his work. It's breaking my heart to see it."

Mike admits that on top of the betrayal, he has fears about his future. "I always said I wanted to go back to school and teach history. But now I don't know if that will satisfy me. I was proud of the job I did. People respected me. I am going to miss that so much. I know I'm not 'Mike Lancaster, corporate executive,' but without my position I'm not sure who I am."

Mike's situation draws into bold relief how work becomes woven into men's egos and self-esteem. There is no equally valuable alternative in Mike's mind to what he has been doing for a quarter of a century. Even in the face of a new kind of freedom, Mike feels he needs and wants the work to complete him. He is like the Gilded Age characters in Edith's Wharton's *The House of*

Mirth. "The doors stood open," she observed. "But the captives had forgotten how to get out."[11]

I Am Not My Father (or Am I?): Questioning the Roles

Forty-year-old Andy Rosenthal, an editor at *The New York Times,* is all too aware of the conundrum in which Mike has found himself. Andy, like many of his baby-boom contemporaries, is trying to figure out how to live his life in the face of the twin pressures of old messages and a work environment that hasn't changed since his father's time. Not only that, Andy wants to have a good career *and* a good life. He doesn't want to define himself by what he does or have his work and his ego (in the best sense of the word) inextricably wedded together.

Andy typifies his generation. Research has shown that the children of the "Organization Man" of the 1950s have very different values about their work than those of their fathers. Less competitive, more cooperative, and concerned with their families and communities, they want a different relationship with their work.[12] It's not that they don't want to work hard, but like Andy, they don't want to be slaves to their jobs. They, like Andy, know all too well the messages they received as boys about what made a man worthy or not.

Growing up, Andy understood clearly that as a man, he had a definite role to play in this culture. "You had to work and you had to succeed and you had to be, if not rich, then famous," he recalled. "In my family I had a father who had a very high-

229

powered career and a mother who was totally devoted to two jobs: raising three boys, and promoting my father's career." When, after thirty-eight years of marriage, Andy's parents divorced, he watched his mother go through a profound loss. "She is seventy-one and has done a lot of really great things in her life, but she feels like it's all been wasted." Andy was determined to live his life differently. After his first marriage didn't work out, he feels his values shifted from "thinking I was going to be happy ninety percent from my job and ten percent from my personal life to thinking I had to have a life outside of work I found fulfilling and rewarding and that wasn't related to whether or not I became executive editor or the emperor of Siam." Andy married again, to an attorney, and a year or so later they had a son. And with the birth of his child Andy found that he was suddenly in the midst of a pitched battle with all the old roles and instructions.

Part of not living his life based on his work meant, for Andy, being a good father and taking on a great deal of the responsibility for the care of their son. After his wife went back to work, they alternated days in which one of them would have to leave work earlyish to get home. "On the days when it's my turn, I just have to stand up and walk out the door, even if I'm in midsentence. I feel very complicated about that. I feel good in a sense—that I'm fulfilling the responsibilities that I think are important and that I'm meeting my commitment to my child and to my wife and that I am taking seriously what I said I was going to do. But at the same time it makes me very nervous, as it has been trained into me that work is a higher calling than fatherhood and that I am abandoning my higher calling for my lower calling. I am walking out the door in the middle of a bunch of responsibilities, and I can't get it out of my head that if the work exists, then I have to do it. Because that's what I've been taught. I'm trying not to value myself that way. I'm trying to change my mind, but it's very hard. Because part of the work ethic I was given was—you just do it."

Andy admits that his great fear about having a child was always that he would not have the strength to push work away and focus on him—that he would end up being a father like his own father. When Andy's son was born, he discovered firsthand how much subtle pressure there was for him to be just that. He found that "apart from my friends, there's not a lot in society that tells you that it's okay to be a father first." At work Andy found people, although outwardly supportive, commented on the length of time (two weeks) that he had spent away from the office when his son was born. "Nobody called me up and said, 'You have to come back to work.' But the message was fairly clear when I came back that this was a bad thing. People couldn't just come out and say, 'What are you? Some kind of lazy fool? What kind of man are you, anyway?' One man said to me, 'What were you doing during those two weeks? Standing by the crib and gazing adoringly at your son?' The message there was 'Spending time at home is not valuable. Spending time at work is valuable. And you're a wimp.' "

Still, Andy decided to place his principles on the line. A month or so later he took another three weeks off, even though his company does not give paternity leave. "I wanted to establish that it is possible to take time off. That it is possible to be a male person with a big career and take time off to stay home with your kids. Because a lot of my colleagues are having babies here, I

231

wanted to be clear to them that if they wanted to take time off, they could do it. That it is ridiculous to set things up so that men feel like they can't take time off. Not even productive. Why would you want to have a group of guys sitting around moping because they haven't had time to bond with their babies? They aren't even doing their work right."

These principles, however, had a flip side for Andy. They came at a cost to him. He found that if he was going to take time off, leave at a reasonable hour, he probably wasn't going to become the big success he had been raised to be. "Why do I have to make the choice between being a successful person at work and being a successful father?" he asked with full understanding that working mothers ask this question almost every day. "Maybe it's not possible to be king of the hill and a good father. So maybe you wind up making a choice. You make it two thirds the way up the hill and wind up being perfectly happy there." Easier said than done when a man judges himself by how much of his potential he has realized in his career.

As much as Andy was able to make some peace with his ambitions, he was unprepared for his ambivalence about being the provider. After all, he had married a woman who worked and made a good income. After a few months back on the job his wife began to think about staying home with the baby; Andy found he had very mixed feelings. While he understood her desires, he found himself deeply divided on the issue. "I always said I didn't want to marry my mother—that I wanted to marry a career woman with her own identity—which I defined as a job. Yet, now that we have this baby, I think it would be fine if she wanted to stay home. I actually don't know how I feel about this. To some degree it worries me. I'm afraid that it will feed all the parts of me that will easily accept the idea that I am just a working individual and not a whole person and I'll just settle into that role—that my wife and kids would become a unit apart from me, one that I will come home and visit. The male-provider role is worrisome for me too. There's anger and frustration associated with it. I tried so hard to be a liberated man and now I feel that I have to be my father. It's infuriating. I spent so much time learning to view women as equals and now it's like 'You're turning into a girl again.' I know these are irrational thoughts and I don't really mean them, but they are real." Andy feels that if his wife does decide not to continue her career for a while, they will have to work very hard not to settle into roles they don't really like. Andy doesn't want to be reduced to breadwinner at the cost of being an outsider to his own family.

And it's not just the roles that concern Andy—there's the question of money. "We had a lifestyle based on being as unconcerned as possible with our finances. We bought cars and motorcycles and went on expensive vacations. We live in a nice house. If my wife stops working, either our lives will change or I will have to pursue an even bigger job," he says, and he doesn't like either option particularly. One represents less security and comfort and the other less time and life outside of work. Andy resents that those are the available choices. After years of trying to value himself more broadly than by the job he performs, fatherhood has thrust all the old values back in his path. He is having a hard time thinking that to be a good father means that he probably won't end up where he would have without a family. But he knows, too, that there is a critical difference between him and the older generation. Unlike his father, who lived through poverty, the Depression, and World War II, he is part of a generation that feels it has the birthright to ask questions. Andy may not be able to completely avoid the old roles, but, like his contemporaries, he can begin to ask challenging questions without social censure. He knows he is part of a society where he can ask of himself, "At seventy, looking back over my life, am I going to be happier with my wife and kids? Or because I had a job with a big title?"

By valuing his family and his work equally, Andy is taking the first steps in a revaluing process that will ultimately break work's determining dominance over his life and self-worth. He and his friends, who are also questioning their roles, are beginning to inch away from their fathers' lives and value system. On a fundamental level they have to shake the foundation of their lives in order to broaden their options in life. As these men introduce (on an equally valuable basis) more traditionally "female" concerns and values into the discussion, they start a process that results in changing not only their predetermined roles but also the way the business itself works.

Cultural Resistance

This kind of revolutionary thinking breeds strong reactions. Moving away from the equation "good provider equals good man" means going against most of the cultural instruction men get about being a man. Men still work in a world where a majority of their male peers think that work is, on balance, fine the way it is. It is very important to emphasize that not every man wants things to change. For many men (and increasingly many women) work still represents a retreat. "Work is men's world. And once the boundaries are blurred, they lose their hegemony. Work for many men is still about closing the door on that messy, nasty undisciplined world at home," comments Letty Cottin Pogrebin. Of course almost no man will admit to this as it appears to cast him in an unflattering light. But many men say it in other ways. They say that their wives are better at taking care of the kids, more patient, more forbearing. For other men like Ron, a sales director of a magazine company, work is fulfilling and exciting enough to compensate for seeing his kids only a few hours a day. He explains that he and his wife are more comfortable with the traditional roles—not because of tradition, but because of who they are as individuals. They both love their work, but Ron doesn't think he's cut out to be a full-time father. He loves what he does and feels that his more than twenty-year career has borne fruit. When he married and had children, work started to mean something different. But unlike Andy, having kids simplified and clarified things for Ron. "It all changed when I became a father. Until then Jessica worked. We had no responsibilities, we had lots of money. Not much was on the line. But after our first kid was born, we agreed that we wanted one of us to be home and raise him. It just happened that Jesse wanted to do it and I didn't. It could have been the other way around. But I get a lot of satisfaction out of making money now. My ambition has increased and I've never enjoyed work more. I'm proud of the fact I can give my family a good life. Besides," he says, "there are real benefits to coming home at the end of the day and not having to be the authority all day long. I get to amuse my kids."

But even men like Ron feel they are working more from choice than from obligation. While he acknowledges they need money, he also realizes that the income could have come just as easily from his wife as from him. They chose a traditional arrangement. Had both wanted to work, they might have been forced into making some difficult concessions. The exclusivity of the male-breadwinner role may have broken down, but men still relish it for the sense of purpose and contribution it provides. There's not much incentive to change things if seventy-five percent of it is working well. And as long as women continue to do most of the work of the home, most of work will still work for men. Besides, for those men who have moved their lives away from a work-centered life, they are all too aware of the difficulties.

No one knows this better than Peter Martin, a former Boston-based newspaper editor. Peter and his wife, Cathy, decided to move to a university town in the midwest so that Cathy could take a tenure-track position teaching in an excellent department. "We moved out here with the understanding that she was going to be the primary breadwinner and I was going to be the primary caretaker," Peter recounts. "Philosophically, I had no problem with that. I approved of it. I embraced it. I was proud of it. In practice, though, it has created problems." Peter and Cathy are very honest with their concerns and are particularly afraid that honestly addressing the problems of defying gender stereotypes will play into the hands of the backlash. They both are extremely careful to state that their arrangement is a work in process, not an example of why it can't be done. But their experiences amply demonstrate the nature of society's and even their own resistance to such revolutionary cultural change.

236

"I scare people," Peter says. "I go in and do PTA work at my daughter's school one day a week and I get strange looks from parents. I can see that they are thinking, *What is that man doing here?* I think some people think I'm a child molester. Others give me more credit than I deserve—like I'm a saint or hero. Obviously, I'm neither of those things. But they can't figure out what I'm doing and why I'm not in an office somewhere."

It's not just his community that looks at Peter askance. "Both my parents and my in-laws are horrified by my life, each in their own ways," he says with resigned good humor. "Cathy's parents certainly expected her to marry a good provider. Don't get me wrong; she was expected to work too. She was raised in as feminist a household as one was likely to find in that era. But her parents certainly expected that Cathy's work would be secondary and that she would not have to worry about being the primary breadwinner." Not only that, Peter thinks Cathy herself is surprised to find this so.

"Though we never said so out loud," Cathy says in a separate interview, "we both came into this marriage with a rather traditional idea that he would probably make more money than I would, be more successful in conventional terms. I even think I picked a career where I thought I could do something interesting and support myself to a certain degree but also have flexibility. My mother worked part-time and my father had the full-time role. That was part of my inheritance." For Cathy and for Peter the fact that she makes more money than he does in his new freelance writing career bothers neither of them per se. It's just that they don't have enough money, period. Her academic salary can't comfortably support the family, and because of where the college is located, there aren't many jobs for Peter.

Cathy's biggest worry is that somewhere down the line, Peter will say, "What have I done with my life?" and regret the decisions they made. She ventures, too, that she is somewhat divided in her feelings about her life. On the one hand she is pleased that their principles have driven their countercultural arrangement—she is happy that her daughter will grow up with strong, nongendered examples of her parents' roles; on the other hand she admits that she feels she has a set of expectations that weren't met. That she doesn't feel taken care of and she doesn't even want to be the one who provides health benefits. "Very simply, why don't I have a nicer lifestyle? In retrospect," she observes, "I expected it was going to happen through my husband. Unless I'm kidding myself, I don't feel let down by him—I think, actually, he's been very bold. It's just that I want my daughter to have new clothes and be able to go to private schools. And I really worry that at some point in the future, Peter will regret having traded his career for my professional happiness. That he will say, 'I threw it all away for this?' "

Peter says he has no real concerns about having left the career path; ironically, it's Cathy who is most worried. She admits that she is still influenced by the cultural dictates about what satisfies men even if she doesn't believe in them intellectually. She doesn't want Peter to miss experiencing conventional success in his life. She also doesn't really want to be the primary financial support all her life. She worries that her daughter will be the one who pays the price for their living out of the sphere of conventional success. In the face of those fears it becomes difficult to appreciate the unvalued side of the equation—that their daughter will have grown up without the example of fixed gender roles and that she will have spent an equal amount of time with both her mother and her father.

For Peter and Cathy, operating outside of convention has allowed them both to clearly see the cultural baggage they not only confront in others but carry within themselves. They know that the pull of the expected roles' values is fierce. It still precludes most men from participating in any life other than the traditionally masculine. "There is too much of a price for men to pay if a man elects a nontraditional choice," Pogrebin observes. "He gets called a wimp, he loses his place in line. The men don't sacrifice money for time, because they will get zapped."

Thinking Outside the Box

For all their extremely sincere questioning and experiments Andy, Ron, and Peter are still thinking about their lives within the confines of a box whose walls, floor, and ceiling are made up of the culture's prevailing beliefs about work and masculinity. Their assumptions about what constitutes success and mediocrity and failure are still much like those of their parents. Even Peter, who is quite intentionally flaunting convention, says he has given up trying to be a success. What he hasn't done is to redefine success on new terms that suit his life. But without a group of like- and open-minded adventurers, doing otherwise is almost impossible. Peter says that there are other male "trailing spouses" where he lives, but any attempt to discuss the psychological or even logistical problems of having a career from their isolated location quickly dwindles into surface chitchat. None of the men is accustomed to trying to solve his problems within a supportive community. They still operate like lone wolves. Not having a successful career carries enough of a shameful tinge that these men remain apart from each other, reluctant to discuss what makes them unhappy in their lives.

If men want to begin to develop a broader definition of success, if they want to move away from the box, they need only look as far as the nearest women in their lives to help them with an alternative model. For women truly know the limits of the success culture. As perpetual outsiders they see much more clearly how much of the way they work is unnecessary. Women have this clarity precisely because they go to work every day in a world designed to meet men's needs, not women's. "Very few women buy into the system completely in the way the guys do," says Anna Quindlen. "I think many more women put on the camouflage to get by, but at a certain point in their lives they say to themselves, *Work is what I do, but it's not who I am.* Whereas men are still really invested in a work-is-everything kind of thing." And it's hard to get the desire, no less the ability, to creatively imagine a different work world when most of it still works.

But a few things are propelling men toward a new way of looking at who they are and what they are worth. As the jobs on which they have depended become less and less secure, the question of choice in work is introduced into the discussion. They see former peers building their own businesses (more out of necessity than virtue, initially, but they are proceeding nonetheless). They see the women in their lives forging new relationships with their work either in terms of hours or location, and earning incomes as good as or better than theirs. As men like Andy strive to be more a part of their families, they are understanding the painful trade-offs required. And as men start to experience some freedom from the economic burden of masculinity, it's beginning to force them to think about work and success in different terms.

Added together, all these changes work to create meaningful choices for men—not just between career success or a personal life but in what constitutes success itself. The door to redefining and revaluing men's lives opens a crack. As long as men and women have thought about their lives within the narrow confines of the conventional success box, men have resented women for their putative ability to choose, while women have resented they've been made to do so. Letty Cottin Pogrebin remembers that when she was writing *Growing Up Free,* she interviewed a little boy who said, "Girls are lucky; they get to wear skirts *or* pants." "There was this perception by this little boy that girls had more privileges because they had choices. But no man wants to wear a skirt; it's not something men desperately want. I don't know too many men who want to stay home full-time, they want someone they trust to stay home full-time. They may want the income of the wife but if they don't need it, they are just as happy to have their wives stay home. Men are still quite comfortable about that. But women aren't comfortable with the choice, they are apologetic in the same way that women in the fifties and sixties were apologetic when they worked outside the home." Once we step out of the box, the choices start to look entirely different. The "nonwork" values immediately become part of the discussion. Our definition of what is successful and valuable be-

241

gins to expand to include more of the things in life that go on outside of the glass towers and factories while the sun is up. All of the things that we have, for years, allowed to remain separate and unequal.

As long as we stick to the old roles and definitions of success, we are necessarily left with only two choices—either we work or we go home. But in accepting those alternatives we miss the real issue, which is that the choices themselves reflect an outdated and artificial division of human life. The either/or nature of our options is nothing but a hangover from another era, and it suits neither men nor women anymore. "I think the transformation that has to happen is not 'either/or' but 'and,' " comments Gloria Steinem. "It isn't that we are either inside corporations or outside with our own businesses transforming values and patterns. We have to do both. And, indeed, we would anyway because women need work." As men lose their work or see their peers break down the all-or-nothing forms of work, it gives them permission to imagine (with dignity) a whole, more balanced life. It allows men to transform their sets of values about themselves to include all of life that the workday excludes.

The Gifts of Transformation

External events may be forcing men to seek alternatives, but there are powerful internal incentives at work as well. As Warren Farrell says, "What's in it for a man is that when he discovers his children, he discovers what life is about. He is directly connected to love, whereas before he was indirectly connected to love. The

242

problem with the male system was that the more money he produced for the people he loved, the further away he had to be from
the people he loved. That's what I call the male tragedy. The
incentive for the men's revaluing of their lives and roles is that
now they will be directly connected to love. A man will be appreciated for the meal he cooks, not depreciated for being away from
home while the meal was being cooked."

Gloria Steinem concurs. "What's killing men is the masculine role. If you take out of the death statistics those men whose
death could reasonably be attributed to the stress of work and the
masculine role, women and men would have close to the same life
expectancy. So this is not a bad deal," she concludes. "You get to
be a full human being instead of hating your 'feminine' qualities,
and distancing yourself from women because they awake these
qualities within you. And you even live longer."

Although this perspective seems to come from a certain deep
maturity, many young men in their twenties clearly see the wisdom in valuing more equally all the options in their lives. They
are building futures for themselves that hint at a deep difference in
their value systems. They clearly see that building a life on the
assumption that work will always be there is a risky, almost insane,
proposition. These young men and women grew up, too, seeing
their mothers work. They came of age believing that the sexes
were equally capable. For this group there has been a drawing
together of the personal and professional worlds. The wall that
separated work and home, which was built along gender lines,
appears to be coming down.

Consultant Janet Andre reports that she is seeing many "Gen
X" men who are saying that their personal life is as valuable to

them as professional achievement. She feels that "the women are influencing the men. I have a twenty-eight-year-old friend who went to one of the military academies. He has a military career. He recently married a high-achieving woman who is now getting her CPA. He now has a challenging assignment, after which, he says, he is considering getting out because his wife can't have a career if he stays in and she wants a career. That's the deal they made before they got married." Besides, Andre says, her friend acknowledges that his wife is much more ambitious than he is. He is more interested in teaching or politics and government. He would rather that she be the high-powered business type. "This is a kid who went to a tough, elite school," she emphasizes. "He's very smart, a high achiever, but she has had a big influence on his life because of her own self-confidence. And it has freed him to be who he wants to be." Andre feels that by the time her friend and his wife get to their mid-thirties, they are not going to have to face the either/or choices that men and women have to face with their lives and their careers. "In order to get talented people companies are going to have to drop their sexism," she says, "and recognize that the work can be done differently. The absolute system based on a male who spends very little time with his children and has a complete support system at home is a dinosaur. It's like school closing in the summer. We have a whole school system built around having the summer off to tend the crops and kids can't even work because of child labor laws. A lot of these senior guys want to be there for their kids now. A lot of the twenty-year-olds want to arrange their lives differently. All this is going to force huge change."

The workplace is not going to change, however, until a critical mass of men demands that it change. And for that to happen, what a man considers valuable about himself and his life has to undergo a revaluation. The women's movement could happen quickly because it didn't change the values of the success culture; it strove to make them equally available. But what now we define as valuable must be broadened. No real change is going to happen until it is as estimable for men to do the traditional work of women as it is for women to do the work previously reserved for men. And we are probably a generation or two away from that moment. "Until men are raising babies and children as much as women are, until men cook what they eat, clean what gets dirty, work won't change," comments Gloria Steinem. "I still get young women in audiences standing up asking, 'How can I combine career and family?' I always tell them, 'You can't until men are asking that question too. You can't do it all by yourself. You can't be superwomen, it's impossible. You have a right to have a partner and a society that behaves as if families matter.' "

There is a shift happening in the balance of power in the workplace. Not just between the sexes but also between the generations. It can wipe away the old, punitive ways we work. It can begin to create management practices that work for the people of today, not forty years ago. It's in men's best interest to stop working by the unwritten rules. If it's true that men today value their lives outside of work as much as women do—and research proves it is—then they have to join women's fight to reconstruct the way we work and create a new, broader definition of success. But as long as family and personal-life issues appear to be the province of women, nothing will change. These concerns will stay on the margins of work's agenda. Men are beginning to see that there are enormous psychological, emotional, and physical rewards in store for them if work changes. They will get to live their lives, know their children, contribute to their communities. They can have a deeper, broader sense of identity and self-worth founded on more than what they do. Men and women both have the need of and the right to stimulating work and rewarding personal lives. Together, we can create the necessary changes.

CHAPTER 10

Balance and Meaning

JULIA, A TWENTY-ONE-YEAR-OLD BAR-
nard College senior, says she wants a job that's meaningful and
exciting. Something in public policy, maybe—or media. She
hasn't decided. But she is very positive of a few things, so much so
that she almost takes them for granted. Julia is sure that whatever
job she tries to get, she will have equal access to employment.
She's confident that she's as capable as any man and that she will
be paid as well. Julia believes she will have a family one day and
that her partner will share equally in the housework and child
care. She doesn't expect to spend her life working in one area or
that she will work for forty years in a corporation. Job security for
Julia means having portable skills, and she doesn't think that having a successful career will take care of her any more than she
believes a man will. In her opinion business has no interest other
than the business of business. To Julia, having a career is important
and a very key part of who she will become. But, as she says, she
isn't going to put all her eggs in one briefcase. Julia has come of

age knowing leaders who only seek cuts, not expansions, a world of downsizing and reengineering, not of growth and endless promise.

It never crosses Julia's mind that she won't work. But she also doesn't believe that work is everything in life. She wants to work hard but not be a slave to it; whatever she ends up doing will be important to her but not defining. She's more concerned about having a job that's meaningful than one that's powerful. What she's looking forward to isn't so different from what I wanted at her age—independence, challenge, freedom, love, and contribution. But I think she knows something about these things that I didn't then—that they can come from many different places and along many different paths. While Julia has the same picture of conventional success available to her as I did, that image is, to her, just one of many socially acceptable possibilities. Because career success no longer promises security and station, Julia has other options that are equally appealing. She doesn't look to a career or a man to give her a place in this world—she even laughs at the question. I wonder what my mother would make of Julia; I think she is highly evolved. Julia already understands in her early twenties what I am just now grasping at forty-one. I wonder what she'll think when she's my age.

Julia isn't prepared to give up her very sturdy sense of who she is to get ahead in her career. She believes, as do others of the generation now coming into the work world, that the power to have a good life is located within her, not in institutions. Her friends have learned by watching their parents that corporate loyalty no longer exists and that successful careers are too often bought with long hours and tremendous stress. This understanding has given Julia's generation a kind of willingness and ability to invent new rules; there seems to be a freedom and fearlessness about their future. They are already creating a generation—not gender—gap at work.

The women starting their careers today aren't prepared to trade their private beliefs for public success. Marie Wilson remembers speaking at the 1996 Feminist Expo and being asked by the young women in the audience what she and other women her age felt they had given up to get where they were. In response Marie told them the story of the woman executive who'd always wanted to be a singer. When standing in front of a group at the first "Take Your Daughter to Work Day" a girl asked her to sing them a song—which she did. She belted out "The Way We Were." As she sang, she cried for the loss of the singer who lived inside. "Well," said Marie, recalling the reaction at the Expo, "it hit me profoundly. What girls are asking of us is 'What parts of ourselves have we cut off?' And they are urging us to bring those parts back. It's all about bringing ourselves back. I said it a few times, and I saw some of the women in the audience had started crying. It was a little weird, really, a little scary—but very real. I saw so clearly that's what we're all struggling with—bringing our whole selves into this world. It touched these girls and it touches me. Because we're all trying to figure out how to do that and we don't have systems that allow it. As a result so many of us are sitting on so much of ourselves every day. And these young women—they got it."

The women in the class of 1977 weren't thinking about what we had to trade for success when we left college—we were thinking about the success itself. Not for its own sake as much as for the very legitimate and powerful reasons of equality and of personal freedom. But we didn't really question the system we thought would give us this control over our lives, only its exclusivity and its bias and discrimination. We were cocksure that we could and would do any job a man could do, and we set our sights on breaking into the ranks of business previously reserved for men. And some of what we got was truly wonderful. And some of it truly wasn't.

Now we are faced with making changes if we want to "bring ourselves back," if we want to grow. That means we will have to challenge and depart from the established picture of success—the one that has brought us to the point where we can now question it. We know any departures entail risking an entire social, if not economic, system of rewards and privileges. We find, however, that we are clinging to one system of privilege with one hand while trying to hold on to who we are with the other.

If we sought alternatives, we were often met with external resistance and internal fear. We found ourselves settling for too little in the quality of our lives—or we had great lives but not enough time to live them. We concluded that the costs and benefits needed to be recalculated to include what we had postponed, brokered, ignored. "Achieving the 'American Dream' is something that's becoming more and more costly," Juliet Schor points out. "What people have to give up to get it is increasing in terms of time, in terms of a feeling of security, in terms of the humiliations of the workplace. All these things quite naturally lead more people to drop out or reject it." We're seeing that things just aren't going to balance out on their own. The silence, the petty politics, the macho work habits, are the cockroaches of the work-place—they are very, very hard to kill.

Julia's generation doesn't believe in the work promises we believed in. They aren't saddled with the pictures of and reverence for success as we were. Just as we rejected the Talcott Parsons 1950s model of the world—the one in which women are supposed to feel and men are supposed to act, the one where women get their identities from men—the next generation has rejected the notion of getting our identities through our work. To them work is simply what they do. In an article on the corporate recruiting of Gen X-ers, *Wall Street Journal* columnist Sue Schellenbarger observed that "while baby boomers have typically kept silent on life-balance matters for fear of being seen as 'uncommitted to the job,'[1] these new recruits see no point in pulling punches." Unwilling to work the way their parents worked, they headed their question list to future employers with quality-of-life issues. They simply weren't interested in the long hours or inflexible structures. They don't want to go to work in a world with an uneven power relationship where the corporation holds the cards. They don't want to miss their kids the way their parents missed them. They have a different definition of success than we have.

As twenty-two-year-old Sarah Schroeder said, "Work is important to me and I really want to do my best. But that's not what I'm working for. I'm working to be able to afford the other values in life."[2] Sarah is an engineer and someone is going to need to hire her. Whoever hires Sarah will hire her values. This is the starting point for the next generation; this is what they have learned by watching us. Just as we wanted more opportunity and more control over our lives than our mothers had, this next generation demands more control over how they work. Maybe because they don't have the same assumption of plenty we had, their agendas *begin* with the quality of their lives. If this generation has broadened the definition of a successful life to include the "other values in life," so can we. Better late than never.

Women like Julia are coming of age at the tail end of what was, undeniably, the greatest social revolution of the twentieth century—the change in the lives of women. The transformation in our lives in a short thirty years has been staggering. While we haven't finished the work of making work an equal opportunity for women, we have come a long way. "What we're working toward now," says Anna Quindlen, "is a completely new paradigm in the way people live—not women, people in general. What we're seeing is the shift from an equality-based revolution to the second stage which says, 'We want parity, we want equality, we deserve it and we will have it. But once we've got it we want to humanize the way the whole world works.' " That "humanizing" means finding a balance between the inner and the outer. The material and the spiritual. The family and the individual. And it translates into a very different way of working.

The Blessings of Broken Promises

I clearly remember the day when I surrendered my fight to make my work work for me. In retrospect what triggered it was a pretty minor event. I'd been out of town on a business trip and I returned to find that some ads for our lead book had been canceled without my consultation by the president of one of the two divisions for which I was publisher. I didn't report to this man, but he still had overall accountability for the profits. It was an awkward arrangement at best. While his actions were fiscally responsible, I saw canceling the campaign as a shortsighted decision; this was the only book for which we had any hopes of commercial success in the season; and we desperately needed the revenue it promised. The decision also invoked a political situation; only one of us could have the final say over the publishing program, and I quickly gleaned that I was now in a "him or me" situation. I knew the incident wasn't personal. This man, a veteran of many different administrations, had been rejecting almost every move I made the way a host body rejects a transplanted organ. His was almost an instinctual reaction, really, based on his best information about how to survive. He wasn't at all a bad man, just a man who had learned to hold on to his power, no matter what.

I had been back for all of one hour when a woman who I knew liked to hedge her bets with management came in to my office to see how I was taking the news. Frankly, I think I disappointed her by not getting angry, not vowing to fight the decision. She, like others I've encountered, seemed to get a perverse feeling of superiority when someone else was down. I wasn't above having done that myself at certain points over the years. But in that moment I suddenly knew I couldn't play the baroque power game anymore. It wasn't even a voluntary decision; I was done. The realization frightened me beyond measure.

I knew I would no longer be effective if I didn't play the game. People would take my lack of fight for no "balls," no gumption. I also thought some very bad publishing would come out of it. In my experience publishing depends on the push and

253

pull of an advocacy process. If there was no resistance from those in my shoes, many expenses—some of which were quite sound investments—would end up cut. It takes a lot of energy to work that way, and I suddenly ran out of my reserves. I decided it was best to quit and let someone else with more fire and desire play the game. I knew it wasn't going to do me or them any good if I stayed.

Talking with my husband that evening, we discussed the ways in which I felt that the company had breached the terms of the contract under which I agreed to work there. But there was a larger transgression, a more meaningful one to me, anyway. And that was in the contract I had made not just with this job, but with my career in general. My unspoken deal was that I would give my career the very best I had to offer; in return I wanted the opportunity to make a difference and go as far as my abilities would take me. I wanted to be respected and recognized for my contributions—not just financially, but spiritually. I wanted to know I made people's lives better, that I'd helped books get read. When I started, I was more than willing to trade four decades' worth of daylight hours for the identity I would receive from my work, from having been a "someone." But in the end, I was faced with loving my work but not the system in which I did it. I felt betrayed by a relationship that I had placed at the center of my life. That promise of recognition may have been realistic for my father when he began his career, but it was no more than a shadow by the time I ended mine. The promises I believed work had made me were ones no one had ever really agreed to in the first place. But with each fresh disappointment my work zeal sank lower, until it had nowhere else to go.

In retrospect that day of the canceled ad was one of the highlights of my career. That was the day the balance within me shifted and I started to look for work on my terms, not others'. I started to take responsibility. I started, at last, to make a new contract with work, one that made sense for this brave new work world.

"Thank God I ultimately didn't get what I wanted." Ellie laughs. "If I had, I'd still be in there swinging with the big boys. I would have missed so much; I had no idea." Not that leaving her prestigious financial institution was a picnic for Ellie—she went through a lot of doubt. "Did I do the right thing? Could I support myself? Would I end up a bag lady on the street? Who was going to give me a pension? Would I get clients? Why would they come to me, not my former employer?" The questions went on and on.

"I've had to weather lots of bad days," Ellie continued. "That's when I've really missed not having a built-in work community. But on the whole most of my fears turned out to be bogeymen, nothing else." Had Ellie listened to those fears, the church in her neighborhood would have had one less youth leader, and Ellie would never have known which of her strengths came from who she was and which from where she worked. Ellie credits that day in her boss's office when she saw the unfair bonuses with the beginning of a whole new way of living. Changing her life may have had its painful moments, but Ellie says that without question it has been the best thing that has happened to her. "I feel free on a really deep level now. It's not just that I work to the level I want, not the level everyone else is at, it's that I have a power over my life I never thought possible. Even my dad doesn't get to me anymore. It's taken until age forty-five, but I'm in control of my life now. I've finally grown up."

Ellie is still an investment banker. But now she does her deals from a small office near her home. She doesn't make the money she used to make and she doesn't have a title. She has to pay for her own health insurance and to get her teeth cleaned. She had all the trappings of power, and all they did was whisper lies in her ear. Like Alice in Wonderland she drank the magic potion and it made her big. Now she sees those things and the world very differently and she wouldn't trade what she has for anything on earth.

The power that Ellie talks about is a much different power than she would have had if she'd stayed at her financial institution. By now she'd probably be a senior vice president, have a company car, be making the really big bucks. But Ellie has redefined power for herself. Anna Quindlen echoed Ellie's redefinition. When she left *The New York Times,* she said that people told her she was giving up power. "I believe that power is the power to do what you want," she states. "That's my whole impulse in life, to be able to do what I want." That kind of control, that redefinition of power, involves shifting it from the institutions around us to ourselves. It flies in the face of the previous generation's understanding of power; it contradicts our beginning assumptions. So many of us went to work to get power—only to find, like me, like Ellie, like Anna—we had it inside us all along. If we didn't feel let down in our contract with our careers, we would never have had to search for that independent inner power. We would never have had the opportunity to define success for ourselves.

The most important ingredient in many women's attitudes is that they have injected meaning into their definition of success. Mary Perkins, for example, has redefined what she wants. "I would like to believe that every day I live is a good day that has some meaning—either to me or somebody else. And there are still many days that I spend now in this corporate environment where I feel like it's a 'wasted' day. What makes it not a wasted day is that I get to go home and hug my husband and my child. Or I get to do something that excites me intellectually. Some things are a higher order spiritually like being an altruistic person. But on a day-to-day basis it's 'How have I improved myself; how have I improved the world?' That's what I'm talking about. Worth." By reframing what was important to her, Mary took the power over whether she was succeeding or failing back into her own hands. For Nancy, had she not felt betrayed by the system that she thought promised her so much, she wouldn't have looked beyond it. Unhappiness enabled her to stop loading so much of who she was on what she did; the result is that she enjoys the work more. "The politics mean much less to me now that I don't want to be king. Now they're just a waste of time and bad background music. Before, it felt like death threats."

Mary, Nancy, and Ellie have made new contracts with their work as a result of hitting the walls of disappointment and betrayal. But as a result, they have work that has some balance and meaning. Like them May, too, has found new purpose. When I asked her what was on her new agenda for her life, she included happy work. Happy family. Work well done. Work that makes a difference to people. Enough money not to worry. Balance.

Time with her family. Time with her friends. Time with herself. That's not such a different checklist than her first one. The values may not be different, but now May has discovered a way to live by them.

By putting first what's most important to her May has created a very different structure for her life. I don't think she sees what she did in such lofty terms, but nonetheless, that's what happened. When I put the values I learned from my father first, I ended up with a life structured just like his. There may be nothing wrong with that, but it just didn't work for me. Like these women, I didn't set out to reorchestrate my life, just turn the volume down on the discomfort and stress. But the only way I could do that and make it last was to ask myself what was important to me and have the guts to stick by it.

Humanized Work

When I quit my job, I had no sense that I was part of a growing movement of women who were trying to figure out a new way of doing work and living life. At the time I was making a decision against something, not for it. I entered my new life by backing into it. But now that I've had some time to look around me, I can see that the "humanized" second wave of the women's movement is in full force. It's just not terribly organized. And it's not just women. Based on values of balance, quality, and meaning, this group is creating new standards for success, an area at a time. Each woman may have a different individual picture, but the characteristics of the movement are becoming clear:

258

Work That Is Value Driven: In 1992, women-owned businesses employed more people than all the *Fortune* 500 companies. In Canada women business owners are the fastest growing group. Many of these women backed into what they were doing because their work didn't work anymore and because they had an inner vision of the way things could be. Nonetheless, from Sharon Hadary's perspective these businesses are value driven. What is most important to them is providing good working environments, having responsible growth, and incorporating balance, flexibility, and respect in the workplace. "I know one woman who is typical," recalls Hadary, "who had a fifteen-million-dollar business. She employed two hundred employees and she could have easily qualified for the *Inc.* magazine Five-hundred list. But she never bothered to apply. She was more concerned with making *Working Mother* magazine's list of the best small companies to work for." When this same woman was asked by an *Inc.* editorial board how to get more women businesses into the top five-hundred independent companies, the woman looked at the editor who had posed the question and said, "Why would we want to?"

Work That Is Flexible: When the values of balance, quality, and meaning lead part of the work contract, a very different work structure results. Instead of the kind of job flexibility we now see (the special-case, Band-Aid kind, the kind that makes the person exercising the option subject to the professional stigma of not putting work first), job sharing and flexible hours become important ways to hold on to important people with important skills. When good job performance is based on quality, "face time" loses its importance. Successful work stops being the amount a person can do in forty, fifty, or sixty hours a week. Instead, job sharing becomes a real possibility. Building work around the values of community and family means we will have a more porous work environment with more work available from our homes. If we value the quality of the product over the hierarchy and systems that produce it, teamwork will naturally evolve as it has with such success in companies like Xerox or Texas Instruments. And with teamwork comes job sharing and more flexibility in time and place.

Work That Is Sequential: One of the biggest changes in a humanized work world will have to do with making work more circular and jobs more sequential. The one-way traffic of the old success path worked for men who expected to have forty-five years of work with a pension at the end. Since staying in one company is now the exception and not the rule, that uninterrupted climb is more nostalgia than reality. Men and women switch companies and careers constantly. Besides, we are all living longer. And healthier. As Lillian Rubin pointed out, "The extended life span has turned things upside down. It's given us new options. I'm seventy-two years old and I sit around thinking, *When I finish this problem, what am I going to do for the rest of my life?"* Jane becomes visibly upset when someone accuses her of retiring. "I'm forty-five," she sputters. "I'm not going to forget how to be an editor. I just don't want to sit in another glass box and elbow my way through a crowd of people to get to a restaurant at lunchtime and pay them too much. Ten years from now I will still want to work. I just want to take some time to figure out how to get a richer life."

Letty Cottin Pogrebin agrees. "This whole business of amassing experience and never taking your shoulder from the grindstone is a little crazy. We shouldn't be so linear. Maybe a person needs to go in and out of the work place and touch base with real life. Maybe spending a few years with a child humanizes you and makes you a better person when you go back in. Maybe we had better rethink the whole thing." Although many have tried to explain away women's departure from the straight-and-narrow path as a casualty of family, maybe if we see it from a prism of revaluing, we will see that women who want flexibility aren't compromising themselves, but finding new ways to work that expand and contract. These are putting an equal value on that kind of flexibility as they do on the slow and steady accumulation of titles and compensation.

Why Work Will Change

Women have a right to work and women need to work—financially, psychologically, and spiritually. We are now more than 50 percent of the workforce and more than half of the entry-level classes for colleges in the U.S. By our undeniable presence we are changing the way work works; we are coming to work and bringing our needs and values with us. "When women enter this particular system, we bring the private world into the public sphere," says Marie Wilson. "That fact has changed the conversation in the public sphere, because we've brought the private values of women into it; we've brought with us the values of community and home and we don't want that split of public and private. This has led to a renegotiation. Now that women are in public life as politicians, as workers, the values of our private lives become a part of solving this problem."

This renegotiation is becoming only more heated as the mix of workers continues to shift. The U.S. Department of Labor estimates that by the late 1990s two thirds of all the people who enter the workforce in the U.S. will be women, a majority of whom will be in their childbearing years. Anyone who thinks women are going home again had best think again. The presence of women has already started a change in men's values. "Every time a man works collegially with a woman in a way he hasn't before and learns to respect her, that's a kind of social change," comments author Wendy Kaminer. "I think that's happening on a small scale in a lot of places and when you add it up, it adds up to something very significant." The question is no longer "Will work change?" but "How fast?"

The first tidal wave of baby-boom women has now reached farther and deeper into management positions in business than ever before. The work culture we entered fifteen, twenty, and twenty-five years ago is metamorphosing—slowly, to be sure, but steadily. It took a while for the cracks to start to appear because it took a while for us collectively to get to places of influence. We come to these positions armed with expertise our businesses need, and with the personal confidence and perspective that comes with accomplishment and experience. This confidence has made us less afraid, which is changing the tenor and content of the work/balance discussion. Besides, many of us are just plain sick of the way things work. We're coming into management positions, having hit the point of saying, "We did the guy thing and the guy thing sucked!" as Anna Quindlen quipped. We elected into the culture and we can elect out.

In addition to our discontent there are two other very important forces at work which suggest that work as we know it will be radically different in a generation or two: 1) Men now also want the structure to change, and 2) in order to attract and keep the best talent, companies are going to have to acknowledge the importance of balance and contribution.

When I asked Andy Rosenthal what he thought was going to happen in his workplace, his response sums up what all the research quantifies—that men want a more humanized way of working, and that they are carefully watching the women in their home and work lives to see how they are faring. "Right now at the *Times,*" he said, "there are five main news departments, which are all currently headed by men roughly my age with young families. All these men are trying to find balance. All of them are trying to make decisions that value their families over their careers. I'm hoping that eventually, one of them is going to be in charge. Change takes time, but a lot of it you have to find and start within yourself. You have to make the personal choices that if you live in a world in which you cannot spend as much time as you want at home and have the same results in your career, maybe you have to give up some of one or the other." Andy mentions that one of the people he most admires is a reporter in his office who has turned down every offer the paper has made to get her to take bigger jobs. This woman made a decision when her child was born that she was going to go home every night at six-thirty, and her current job makes that possible. Andy realizes that this woman made a conscious choice that cut out some real possibilities for her future, something that may frustrate her in later years when her child is older and she isn't needed at home as much. "But she wants what she's got," he says with evident respect. "It's easier for me to think about doing what she has done than it was for my father. I guess that's progress."

In 1991 a study by the Families and Work Institute showed that twice the number of men under forty said they would forgo raises and advancement for a better home life than had been willing to do so five years earlier. A 1992 study by the same group showed good management, inclusive communication, and what impact work would have on family life were more important factors than the amount of salary in choosing an employer.[3] Stories of men who give up high-powered jobs appear with more and more frequency in newspapers and magazines, paving the way for others to follow with some measure of societal support. Our brothers, friends, and husbands, whose lives are so similar to ours, identify more with our work concerns than they do with their fathers'. As the measure of masculinity starts to detach from the old picture of success, we can start to look forward to real and increasingly rapid change in the culture and structure of our offices.

The final factor propelling change is that companies are starting to see that their businesses' bottom lines will be hurt when talented people either leave or hold themselves back from greater contributions because they don't want to sacrifice their lives for their jobs. The woman Rosenthal mentioned was a source of frustration to the *Times'* management, according to someone else who had worked at the paper. They wanted her talents represented in the highest ranks. They wanted her contributions, her perspective, her experience. But she made a decision that she did not want to work in a way that didn't match her personal priorities. As a result the skills of someone they deeply valued haven't been applied to a higher level in the company. "Our national blindness to the real lives of American men and women today is causing physical and emotional problems and may one day swing a wrecker's ball at the bottom line as well as at the health of American workers,"[4] assert authors Barnett and Rivers. Their study, like the pioneering work of Juliet Schor of Harvard and Lotte Bailyn of MIT, has offered persuasive proof that constructing work around the values of balance, inclusion, and meaning produces healthy, satisfied employees and profits.

To the generation now running our businesses, changing from the unwritten rules to value-based work represents the ultimate threat to control. At stake is a tremendous shift in the balance of power—and the issue is who is going to control work. This shift is already happening, actually; it's an inadvertent by-product of downsizing. What we are seeing around the world is the growth of what Peter Drucker calls "knowledge workers," those of us who carry our expertise with us from place to place, unanchored by the values of a corporation. If a business can't control employees through fear of job insecurity or lack of advancement, it loses control—the control shifts to us. When that happens, we can start to dictate the terms—the terms of balance, the terms of dignity and recognition.

This message will stop seeming so revolutionary and threatening only when the baton is passed from the generation still governed by the visions of the fifties fantasies to the baby-boom generation and the generation beyond us. The transformation we seek for lives of meaning and balance is, as Gloria Steinem pointed out, a transformation of "and," not "either/or." But the values and the behaviors of women and men have to change first; only then will the structures around us begin to reflect what is important to us.

Why This Is Important to More than the Upper Class

At one point early on in this book I stood back and asked myself if this issue of women and work values was one that simply applied to the upper and middle classes—those of us who live with the luxury of choice in employment and some real chance, if not measure, of economic security. Desiring a broader vision than that of my own experience, I went to those women who I felt had some true perspective on how far reaching these issues were. Each had a different slant on things, but each categorically pointed out how important these issues are for all women.

"If we start to create a system of values that does not value people on a hierarchy of how important you are in the world, then you start to help the women who are doing work that isn't traditionally valued," Marie Wilson stated. "By reframing what we value, what we're trying to shift is of real importance to women who are not in 'elite' occupations. When work is not how we get our sense of who we are in the world, we can start to think about how we share work and about different ways to work. For the people who are doing work that we might now consider less valuable, there will be a leveling of the pay, a leveling out of how people get rewarded for what they do. It's kind of a utopian idea, but there's a possibility that it will make work that is less sexy pay more." To do that, Wilson says, we need to interrupt the identity dynamic. "To be a person living in a world where work isn't only what is valued, what's valued is your ability to make friendships or be a part of a community, we have to articulate that. A value isn't a value if it's dead. A value is only a value if people start to say, 'Look at so and so, she has really changed the way she wants to live, I'm so pleased.' We have to really teach people to say it out loud, because if we don't hear it, it's dead. It is silent, it will never change anything. Right now, people aren't saying it and we're going to have to embolden people to say those words."

Gloria Steinem said she didn't feel it was a class-bound issue at all—she hears the same concerns from factory workers and welfare mothers just off the welfare rolls. The values of the workplace don't work for them because, as Susan Faludi pointed out, "the issue of identity through work comes up at every level. For every woman, whether clerk or secretary, to them their work is important. It's the same loss. It isn't just about the paycheck. You can't really separate the two. Part of your identity is that you can support yourself and that you are part of a public world and you are compensated for that. There are nuances from class to class, but there it's still the same issue. People feel erased."

Being recognized for who you are and what you can contribute is not a middle-class concern, it's a human one. It's easier for a group of predominantly white female college graduates to push for changes in the work culture because we have the luxury of believing we are all basically employable. We have the undeniable luxury of living far above the sustenance level. Most of the time it's our lifestyles—not our lives—at stake. When we begin valuing our lives as much as our lifestyles, the changes we strive for today will help all women in all classes in the future. Because all women want to control their lives. All women want to be recognized for all of themselves.

The greatest number of new jobs being created combine the two most proven lethal ingredients in terms of job stress: repetition and low (if not no) control. And these jobs are being filled overwhelmingly with women. If the women at or near the tops of the companies creating these jobs work to change the culture to acknowledge and accommodate the real lives and demands of women, they are only going to help the women in these new, taxing jobs. And maybe, in a better world, the jobs themselves will be restructured.

To Be Continued

Now for the fantasy part of the story: Three quarters of the way through writing this book, I looked up from my desk in the small yellow room tucked behind my kitchen and realized that what I had been doing for the previous nine months was called work. It certainly didn't feel like any work I recognized. Once the publisher and I agreed on the scope of the book, I had enjoyed control over what I was producing. I assigned my own tasks, decided what to do when, and what might be the best way of doing it. Writing and researching and interviewing—while regularly difficult and frustrating—never ceased to engage, stimulate, and energize me. During this entire time I never once had an argument with management, never once felt disrespected or unrecognized. And for close to a year I hadn't had to put on a pair of heels or hose, or upend my life when my child came down with an ear infection. I was being paid to do this. The realization stunned me. I love my work; it works for me.

My new profession has come with definite trade-offs. I swapped the security of a paycheck every two weeks for iffy, irregular income. Yes, I could take the risk, in part because I had a supportive mate who could keep things going. But had he not been around, I had savings I'd been stashing away for just this kind of emergency. I also traded prestige, social status, an expense account, and the day-in-and-day-out community of people I respected and liked to be around. Whatever power I enjoyed as a publisher disappeared the moment the office building's elevator door clicked shut behind me. It was astonishing how quickly the phone stopped ringing. If something had to be mailed, I went to the post office. When my computer ate one hundred interviews, sad to say, I was the technical support. In my new life I no longer made strategic decisions or marshaled resources. Some days I couldn't even get my kid to take a nap.

It took some time to get used to the changes, but after a while I did. Where I ran into serious trouble was with the loss of my old identity. Ironically, for months I felt like a failure rather than someone who had decided to quit. Even with new work I couldn't get past the fact that somehow I had failed to do what I had expected of myself twenty years earlier. Failed because I hadn't stuck it out, done it perfectly. Failed because, though I'd done all the items on my checklist, my life still was missing something big. I failed because my skin never got tough enough, failed because balance eluded me. I failed because I couldn't have it all. I failed because I wasn't a success. At least in the way I had defined success. Even though I was working, contributing, supporting myself, independent, I was having a hard time accepting that what I was doing was valid. I went through the same miserable process of letting go that the women in this book went through. Like them I needed to revisit my assumptions about what made me a valuable person and what I thought comprised a successful life. Revisit them and redefine them all.

I began by realizing that the dream of having it all in a perfect world was just that—a fantasy. More importantly, I stopped holding myself up against its image. I spent way too much of my time measuring my life against my expectations instead of against what was possible. I confused the best that I could do with the best that could be done. And as long as I remained jet-fueled by that elusive picture of perfection, I was continually propelled forward toward that which constantly remained just slightly out of reach. This quest kept me focused on my own shortcomings instead of on those of the world in which I worked. As long as I did that, I remained the problem.

Toward the end of writing this book I came across a book review of Christopher Lasch's final work. In it the reviewer quoted Lasch's observation that there has been "an increasingly narrow identification of the American Dream with the American standard of living."[5] And since that world is no longer expanding, Lasch believed we as a culture have been heaved into a spiritual crisis. In retrospect, Lasch felt, the one "unambiguous success" he and his wife could claim in raising their children in "this unappeasable consumer culture was their 'failure to educate them for success.' "

I don't think my father did me harm in urging me to do whatever I wanted to do. Indeed, I wouldn't change a piece of my life. I think it has all been necessary for me to understand the terms under which I worked for twenty years and to take control of the next twenty. But I did go through a profound spiritual crisis when I honestly confronted the real nature of my discontent—when I clearly saw how much of who I was depended on work I couldn't control. Learning to take charge of my new agenda and revalue my life while living it was a little bit like fixing a car that is not just running but moving. There have been many points where I didn't see where I was going or if I did I questioned the wisdom of the route. I have had moments of profound doubt and sadness. Confusion has been a frequent companion. But in the end I stopped weighing my decisions against those of other women I respected. Doing so forced judgment. And judgment, I realized, was a big part of the problem. We come from a system of success or failure. Of status. Of power. Of hierarchy. This is what I want to move away from. Whatever form my work comes in, I want it to value and respect all of who I am. What's right for one woman or man is not necessarily right for me. Work that works honors all the choices as much as it honors the different parts of our lives.

I look at my son and ask myself, *What am I teaching him about the values of life and work and friends and family?* Does he see balance in my husband's work? Probably not today. In mine? I'm not so sure, but it's closer than it was. Like my father I want the best for my child, this young person of the twenty-first century. I hope

271

the changes we're starting to make in the work culture today will make it easier for him to have a successful life on his own terms. It's the surest way to happiness that I can see. By transforming our present we can give the gift of a balanced and meaningful future to our children. Which, for me, ultimately, is the final picture and the truest measure of a successful and meaningful life.

Notes

INTRODUCTION

1. Betsy Morris, "Executive Women Confront Midlife Crisis," *Fortune,* September 18, 1995, p. 62.

2. While most of the women in the research were of the classic baby-boom age—roughly ages 35–50—it's important to say that those women in their late twenties and early thirties identified very strongly with the feelings and situations their older counterparts described.

CHAPTER 1

1. *Women: The New Providers,* a Whirlpool Foundation Study, Part One, by Families and Work Institute, May 1995, p. 10.

2. Sara Ann Friedman, "Family Values Revisited," *Barnard,* Spring 1996, p. 56.

3. *Women at Work: Executive Summary,* research conducted by *Fortune* and Yankelovich, October 1995, Table One.

4. Barbara Ehrenreich, "In Search of a Simpler Life," *Working Woman,* December 1995, pp. 28, 29.

CHAPTER 2

1. It's important to note that women slightly younger than this group, those twenty-five and up, said that even though they came into the work world as it was shrinking, they still felt so indoctrinated by the need to achieve that they continued forward even in the face of this duality. As one 32-year-old architect said, "We still had the ethos drilled into us that career was all, that making it was the way to fulfillment, but the bloom was off the rose fairly early on. Once you or one of your friends is crisply made redundant, the workplace looks a less nurturing and fulfilling place. But many of us were (and are) too wired into the success culture to give it all up."

CHAPTER 3

1. Rosabeth Moss Kanter, *Men and Women of the Corporation* (New York: Basic Books, 1977, 1993), p. 207.

2. Joseph B. White and Carol Hymowitz, "Broken Glass: Watershed Generation of Women Executives Is Rising to the Top," *The Wall Street Journal,* February 10, 1997, p. A1.

3. Kanter, op. cit., p. 214.

4. Susan Wittig Albert, *Work of Her Own: How Women Create Success and Fulfillment Off the Traditional Career Track* (New York: G. P. Putnam's Sons, 1992), pp. 14, 15.

5. Kanter, op. cit., p. 211.

6. Ibid., p. 228.

7. Mary Pipher, *Reviving Ophelia* (New York: Ballantine Books, 1994), p. 38.

8. *The A Capella Papers,* Canadian Teachers' Federation, Ottawa, Canada, 1993.

9. Gina Maranto, "Delayed Childbearing," *Atlantic Monthly,* June 1995, p. 65.

10. Arlie Hochschild and Anne Machung, *The Second Shift* (New York: Avon Books, 1990), p. 3.

CHAPTER 4

1. Kanter, op. cit., p. 251.

2. T. E. Apter, *Working Women Don't Have Wives* (New York: St. Martin's Griffen, 1995, 1993), p. 31.

3. Gloria Steinem, *Revolution from Within: A Book of Self-Esteem* (Boston: Little, Brown and Company, 1992), p. 22.

CHAPTER 5

1. Anna Quindlen, *Thinking Out Loud: On the Personal, the Political, the Public, and the Private* (New York: Random House, 1993), p. xxviii.

2. Catalyst, New York, 1996.

3. Albert, op. cit., p. xvi.

4. Juliet Schor, *The Overworked American* (New York: Basic Books, 1991), p. 23.

5. Virginia Woolf, "Professions for Women," *The Virginia Woolf Reader,* edited by Mitchell A. Leaska (New York: Harcourt Brace, 1984), p. 279.

6. Albert, op. cit., p. 6.

CHAPTER 6

1. *The 1990 Virginia Slims Opinion Poll: A Twenty Year Perspective of Women's Issues,* The Roper Organization, Storrs, Connecticut, p. 26.

2. *Yearning for Balance, Views of Americans on Consumption, Materialism, and the Environment,* prepared for the Merck Family Fund by the Harwood Group, Takoma Park, Maryland, 1995, p. 20.

3. Schor, op. cit., p. 9.

4. Gary Belsky, "Women Worry More Than Men About Money," *Money,* June 1996, p. 24.

5. Steven A. Holmes, "Income Disparity Between Poorest and Richest Rises," *The New York Times,* June 20, 1996, p. 1.

6. Schor, op. cit., p. 109.

7. Merck, op. cit., p. 1.

8. Schor, op. cit., p. 1.

9. Schor, op. cit., p. 20.

10. *Women's Voices: A Joint Project of the Ms. Foundation and the Center for Policy Alternatives,* New York and Washington D.C., 1992, p. 13.

11. *Yearning for Balance* study, op. cit., p. 14.

CHAPTER 7

1. Pipher, op. cit., p. 26.

CHAPTER 8

1. Bill Carter, "A Farewell to 'ER,' Blood, Guts, and Fame," *The New York Times,* November 21, 1996, p. C15.

2. Ibid., p. C16.

3. Pipher, op. cit., p. 26.

4. A Queen Bee, a personality type drawn by Graham Staines, Carol Tavris, and Toby Epstein Jayaratne in their January 1974 *Psychology Today* article.

5. Lotte Bailyn, Rhona Rappoport, Deborah Kolb, Joyce Fletcher, et. al., *Re-Linking Work and Family*, Working Paper, Alfred P. Sloan School of Management of the Massachusetts Institute of Technology, 1996, p. 9.

6. National Foundation for Women Business Owners.

CHAPTER 9

1. Warren Farrell, "The Human Lib Movement: I," *The New York Times*, June 17, 1971, p. 41 citing the California Gender Identity Center's research.

2. Rosalind C. Barnett and Caryl Rivers, *She Works/He Works: How Two-Income Families Are Happier, Healthier, and Better Off* (San Francisco: HarperCollins, 1996), p. 5.

3. "A Matter of Honor," *Newsweek,* May 27, 1996, p. 24.

4. Barnett and Rivers, op. cit., p. 6.

5. Ibid., p. 49.

6. Ibid., p. 56.

7. Ibid., p. 57.

8. Ibid., p. 6.

9. Ibid.

10. *Women: The New Providers,* op. cit., p. 33.

11. Kennedy's Fraser's essay "Warmed Through and Through," in her *Ornament and Silence: Essays on Women's Lives* (New York: Alfred A. Knopf, 1996), p. 74.

12. Barnett and Rivers, op. cit., p. 144.

CHAPTER 10

1. Sue Schellenbarger, "Work and Family," *The Wall Street Journal,* January 29, 1997, p. B1.

2. Ibid.

3. Barnett and Rivers, op. cit., pp. 62, 65.

4. Ibid., p. 136.

5. Andrew Delbanco, "Consuming Passions," *The New York Times Book Review,* January 19, 1997, p. 8. A review of Christopher Lasch's *Women and the Common Life: Love, Marriage and Feminism,* edited by Elisabeth Lasch-Quinn (New York: W. W. Norton & Co., 1997).

Index